SELF-ESTEEM FOR INTROVERT PEOPLE:

A Survival Program to Overcome Shyness, Improve your Relationships and Develop Social Skills with Cognitive Techniques and Positive Affirmations.

Introduction

Just as the word implies, self-esteem simply means the confidence exhibited by oneself. Confidence can also be likened to fueling out inner capacity to meet or surpass expectations. For instance, people with self-confidence tend to face specific hurdles with unwavering thoughts that the situation is a win-win for them. Even if they fail in particular life challenges, they always have the will to and inbuilt, infused encouragement to try again with the assurance of making a difference. When talking about self-confidence, it is not restricted to a set of people, sex or age group but every shade of human bings.

For instance, students that might have been experiencing some form of consistent academic set-back may have issues with their self-confidence. And the reduced self-confidence may start kicking in due to the adverse reaction or comment they tend to get from their teachers, parents or colleagues based on their not-so-good academic performances. While on the other hand, students that consistently have excellent performance tend to experience increased self-confidence due to the delight that revolves around it.

So, in a nutshell, self-confidence is more about certainty of an event or occurrence as seen from the perspective of an individual. Self-confident make you have the perception that you are capable of handle specific situation. And this confidence may revolve around academics, business, family, and relationships with others, to mention a few. However, for those that have been experiencing some sort of insufficient confidence in themselves, one thing among many others has been found to help. And that making a decision to leave your comfort zone and actually taking that step into the unknown so to speak. Many people have the capacity to do more but have little knowledge about it. But leaving your comfort zone, and placing yourself in the middle of space where you might have been running away from will undoubtedly trigger some willpower within you that you have never thought was there. And with this, your self-confidence will keep developing.

Here are hints to know your possess self-confidence:

Not being pulled back from making specific decisions because of the thought of failure

Not criticizing others around you to make them feel lesser than you are.

Having assure of delivering any target ahead of you.

Having a unique ability to adapt to any situation, whether favorable or not.

Capacity to try new things out

Believing in your ability irrespective if it being small compared to others.

Self-esteem

The word esteem is also used in various ways. For instance, you tend to have someone you hold in high esteem, such that your lookup to them, admire them, and even do something similar to them. But the self-esteem being talked about here revolve around self-worth and self-emotions due to assessment or evaluation of yourself compared to others. A handful of people are in this trap of depreciating self-esteem because they don't appreciate themselves or what they have. However, with the understanding that you are different path to walk in life compared to others, make your see reasons not to look down on yourself. You may have confidence in yourself but still be restricted from making viable progress due to the prevalence of self-esteem. Hence, you need to love and appreciate yourself for who you are, the abilities you possess and your unique ways of approaching situations; then you start experiencing renewed self-esteem.

Here are some hints that can help in identifying positive self-esteem:

Not looking down on others because of their achievement but joining them in appreciating their skill and success

Not engaging in harmful or unproductive discussion. Doing this prevents you from drowning further in the wells of negative self-esteem

Having the capacity to say 'Yes' or 'No' without undue influence from anybody or thing.

Accepting your weakness and strength as they are, and also, doing what is within your power to improve on them.

Possessing the ability to pick yourself up when you fall or fail in some things.

Nonetheless, irrespective of the unique differentiation between self-esteem and self-confidence, they still have a lot in common and can be used interchangeably in certain situations.

In a nutshell, always accept yourself for who you are, without unnecessarily comparing yourself with others. Likewise, have the 'everyone can make a difference' mentality. No one is better than anybody else; everyone has a role to play, so play yours to the fullest.

Chapter 1 - How to protect yourself from energy vampires

Recognize and Protect Yourself from Energy Vampires

Energy vampires are people who can drain a great deal of energy from you. They tend to have problem after problem, and they constantly come to you, asking for more than a reasonable amount of support. As an Empath, you feel into their position, empathize with them, and find yourself feeling personally responsible for providing them with the energy required to do what is needed from you. This quickly turns into a treadmill, where you are constantly running to meet the energy needs of the person but you are never able to fulfill their needs. This is because they are an energy vampire.

In order to protect yourself from energy vampires, you need to teach yourself how to say "no." Learning to say no and stand behind it is important. This is how you can support yourself in feeling confident and protected in saying no. When you say no to an energy vampire, make sure that you consciously say no with your energy as well. Some people will envision their protective shield blocking out the request, preventing the energy from coming into their space altogether. Keeping out the energy of the energy vampire is important. If you let it in, it can begin to create empathic sensations within you that might cause you to change your mind. This is less of a worry when you become stronger in protecting yourself, but early on you are susceptible to changing your mind as a result of this energy.

Recognizing energy vampires and learning how to say no to them will also require you to protect yourself from shouldering any further responsibility. Affirming to yourself that it is not your duty to fulfill other people's needs beyond what you feel is reasonable is important. If you are not doing it out of love for yourself and the other person, you are not doing it for the right person. If you are doing something that extends more of your energy than you can reasonably give, then you are giving too much. Make sure that you educate yourself on saying no and that you consciously clear your energy field from the request as well. This will protect you against the energy, the request, and the energy vampire. You also want to minimize the amount of time you spend around the energy vampire as much as possible and practice setting stronger boundaries with them in regards to what you are willing to listen to and engage with in order to create a stronger sense of protection against the energy vampire. This way, you do not feel like you are constantly in protection mode and you give yourself space to breathe and enjoy life.

Save Yourself from Time Vampires Too

In addition to energy vampires, there are also time vampires. Frequently, an energy vampire may also be a time vampire. However, not all time vampires are energy vampires. Time vampires are people who take up far too much of your time. You may find yourself constantly doing things for them, spending excessive time with them, or investing a great deal of time worrying about them. As a result, they end up taking up far too much of your precious time.

The best way to deal with a time vampire is to limit the time that you are willing to share with them. Decide what your boundary needs to be, set it, and stand behind it. Begin reinforcing it by only giving them the allotted amount of time and then saying no when the boundary is reached. This also counts when you are thinking about them. If you find yourself worrying about the person, say no to yourself and set a boundary with yourself as well. Reducing the amount of time you are willing to spend on a person, especially one that is toxic toward you (whether consciously or unconsciously) can support and protect you.

Even though it is nice to help people and you want to help others feel good in their lives, it is not your responsibility. Have an honest conversation with yourself about why you feel personally responsible for others and then begin to enforce boundaries with yourself as well. Creating these personal boundaries will make it easier for you to prevent yourself from feeling personally responsible for everyone else's needs and feelings. Then, it will become easier for you to say no and protect your time. When you do say no, make sure that you fulfill that time instead with something that is a genuine act of self-love. The more you take good care of yourself, the easier it is to understand why you deserve your time, energy, and attention even more than anyone else. Even if that does not feel natural or "right" to you in the beginning. Soon, you will understand that it is a necessary protection and self-care practice. Not only does it help you feel great, but it will also amplify your ability to help others.

Preserve and Protect Your Energy

It is important that you learn to preserve and protect your energy as an Empath. Knowing how to "tune out" of the world from time to time to give yourself the space to recharge is important. One great way to do this is through getting a high-quality set of noise-cancelling headphones and putting them on when you go out in public or when you are in noisy environment. While you may not be able to do this every time, using them in certain circumstances can support you in staying focused on the energy of the music rather than the environment around you. Consider using music that is uplifting and upbeat so that it actually amplifies your energy, rather than you going out and coming home feeling depleted.

Another way to protect your energy is to begin practicing energetic boundaries. This means that you make yourself unavailable to tune into the energies of those around you unless you give yourself permission to do so. Set the boundary with yourself that you are not going to tune into any energy.

Learning to switch your gift "on" and "off" can take practice, and the best way to do it is just to start. Soon, you will learn to be firm and consistent, and your boundaries will be effortless to uphold. This means that you begin gaining power and control over your Empath gift so that you no longer feel like you are being ruled by it. Instead, you can rule the gift and use it as you need to in order to support you in your life and soul purpose, as well as in leading a quality life.

Shield Your Aura

Shielding is a powerful practice that Empaths use to protect themselves from external energies. This is a form of creating an energetic boundary that can stay in place and keep you feeling protected without you always having to be consciously working toward it. In the beginning, your energetic shield may need continuous conscious reinforcement. Once you become more skilled with it, however, it becomes a lot easier.

The best shield to consider using when you are going out in public, or anywhere that your gift may be overly activated, is called a bubble shield. This shield is created by you envisioning a white light glowing in your solar plexus. This light then grows and grows, purifying your body and energy field and filling it with white light. Let this light grow until it forms a bubble that extends four feet away from your body in either direction, including down into the Earth. This shield is one that, once built, will stay in place as long as you desire. If you feel that your shield is down or you have taken it down by accident, you can always recreate it using the same strategy. Some people even choose to create a new one every morning to support them in staying protected throughout the day. Any time that you feel your energy is being threatened visualize your shield to reinforce it and keep unwanted energies out.

Energy Vampires and Empaths

Kaye is an empath. She has a beautiful soul that lights up her surroundings. She does not only feel other people's emotions, she also absorbs them. When someone is happy, she is also happy. When someone is sad, she is also sad.

Her officemate, Glenda, is a beautiful woman. She has a good life – a three-bedroom house, two cars, two kids, and a good husband. However, she does not seem to appreciate everything she has. She complains about everything in her life.

Kaye feels weak when she is near Glenda. It is as if she is sucking her energy. She feels drained after talking to her.

Glenda is an energy vampire. She is beyond toxic. However, what is an energy vampire? Why do they drain all your energy? How can you spot them?

You see, every interaction with another human being is an energy exchange. Some people (like the empaths) give us good energy, while other people (like the energy vampires) sap it.

Let us say that you just were fired from work and you are really angry and sad. Therefore, you decided to talk to your mom about it. Your mom is warm, welcoming, and loving demeanor calms you down. It gives you hope. It makes you realize that life is not very bad.

Your mother is what we call an "energy-giver". She has this rejuvenating effect. She makes you feel safe and secure.

Now, let us say that you lost your job and you decided to talk to your father. He is not as warm as your mom is. He is a harsh critic. After you told him your problem, he started saying things like "you'll never find another job because you're stupid" and "well, that's expected because you're good for nothing". Your dad, in this scenario, is what we call an energy vampire.

Energy vampires are emotionally immature people who feel like the world revolves around them. They have an underdeveloped psyche, so they feed off other people's emotional and psychic energy.

They are sometimes overly dramatic. They engage in erratic behavior. Some energy vampires are just plain pessimistic. Some of them are harsh critics. However, some of these toxic people are extremely dangerous – sociopaths, narcissists, and even psychopaths.

Here are the common characteristics of toxic people:

You feel sick and tired after talking to them.

Energy vampires are difficult to talk to. They complain and they criticize everything you say. They make you feel stupid.

After you talk to a toxic person, your shoulders feel heavy. It is as if you carried two sacks of rice or two hollow blocks.

They kill your hopes and dreams.

Eleanor wanted to be a ballet dancer when she was young. However, she was from a poor family and her parents cannot afford ballet lessons. Her mother said that dancing is a hobby and not a profession. Therefore, she chose to be a teacher instead.

Even if she is good at her job, Eleanor grew bitter because she did not achieve her childhood dreams.

Instead of lifting her students up, she craps on their dreams. She tells her students that they are too ugly to become a celebrity or too stupid to become an entrepreneur. She would come up with over a million reasons why her students cannot do whatever it is that they want to do.

You would be surprised to know that there are a lot of teachers who think and act like Eleanor. However, toxic naysayers are not only found in the academe. You can find them everywhere. They can be your sister, friends, co-worker, romantic partner, and even your parents.

They say things like:

"Are you sure you have enough experience?"

"I don't know if that would work."

"It's already done before."

"It's unproven."

"I'm not sure if someone would pay for it."

"That sounds dangerous."

"It's going to be difficult."

Most naysayers have not achieved their own goals and dreams. They do not have an inspired existence. They are cloaked in self-loathing, jealousy, fear, and so they project these fears onto other people.

They make you feel bad about your life.

Toxic people will make you feel bad about your life. They make you feel like you are not good enough. They use their passive aggressive nature to make you feel like you are stuck and can never escape your job or your problems.

They only pay attention to you when they need something from you.

We all have that one friend who only calls us when they need a favor. Toxic people only give you attention when it serves them. They will use you and take everything you have until there is nothing left.

They hold grudges.

Joel was married to Diana for 7 years. They have a picture-perfect marriage. They have two kids and they look like they love each other. They seem like they have it all.

One day, Diana talked to Joel. She told him that she is no longer happy with their marriage and that she has been having an affair with her boss in the last two months.

Joel was beyond devastated. He started to stir up drama on social media and made sure that his friends know about Diana's affair.

However, 2 years later, Joel is still as bitter as he was when Diana broke his heart. He has become toxic. He is angry all the time and defames the mother of his children whenever he can. He just cannot let everything go.

Toxic people hold grudges. They bring up your past mistakes to create drama. They just cannot move on. They exude the negative energy that makes you feel weak and dizzy.

They do not take responsibility for their actions.

Nothing is ever their fault. They blame their problems on other people. They do not take responsibility for their actions and their lives.

They are inconsistent.

It almost feels like they have multiple personality disorder. They change their attitude, behavior, and personality to manipulate other people and get what they want.

They are colder than ice.

They are not supportive. They withhold love to manipulate you and get you to do whatever they want.

They lack empathy.

Empathy is a strong indication of a healthy personality. Energy vampires often have no empathy. They have a hard time understanding what other people are going through.

They have a huge ego.

Toxic people often have an inflated self-image. They feel like they are smarter and better than the people around them are. They feel like they know everything.

They are abusive.

Some toxic people are just plain "evil". They can be both physically and emotionally abusive. They would humiliate and bully you. They would force you to give up your power so they can do whatever they want.

Different Types of Energy Vampires

Energy vampires are generally drawn to empaths because of their warmth and compassion. They often feast on empaths' energy.

If you are an empath or a highly sensitive person, you should try to stay away from the following energy vampires.

Drama Queen

Ara is a successful film producer. She is intelligent and has mad writing skills. She has a sharp wit and a captivating beauty. However, she constantly craves for attention and engages in attention-seeking behavior. She has a strong sense of entitlement.

She constantly stirs up dramatic situations. She will manipulate other people. She loves to create gossip just to start a conflict. She loves to pit her friends against each other just for her own entertainment. In addition, she is obsessed about looking and being perfect. She gets hysterical over the smallest things.

Drama queens have zero accountability for their life and behavior. They start gossip just to create drama and conflict.

They like pitting people against each other. They often recruit minions to help them tear down their targets.

These people are not only toxic. They are also shallow. They feel like the world is going to end just because they are having a bad day. They like being the center of attention.

Jealous Jane

Marie has a great life. She is an American living in the beautiful island of Capri. Everything in his r life seems perfect.

However, when she opens her Instagram account, she sees her friends going frolicking in exotic islands like Bali and Maldives. She sees her friends' wedding photos and she felt like she is missing out a lot in life.

She is chronically unhappy and complains about every little thing. She does not appreciate everything she has.

Jealous people carry the heavy, negative energy that is extremely dangerous to empaths. These people have low self-esteem. They are emotionally unstable. They berate others to cover up their feelings of inadequacy.

Temperamental Tom

Albert is a good man most of the time. He is kind and generous. However, he has a short temper. He gets angry over small things and he has a hard time controlling his anger.

When he is mad, he would throw anything he can get his hands on. He uses everyone around him as an emotional toilet. He dumps emotional crap whenever he can.

Temperamental Toms are draining and scary. Regular exposure to these toxic people can lead to extreme emotional trauma.

Manipulating Mark

Manipulating Marks are tricky and deceptive people who will pose as your friend. They will take time to know the things that can make you happy. They will use this information to manipulate you to do what they want you to do.

These toxic people often play the victim. They would exaggerate their personal issues, so you would sympathize with them. They tell half-truths to get what they want.

They will often pressure you or engage in passive aggressive behavior just to get you to see things their way.

Arrogant Arman

Arrogant people see everything as a competition. They believe that they are superior to others and sometimes, too cocky.

These people exaggerate their abilities to make you feel bad about yourself. They constantly brag about their accomplishments. They are often rude and mean.

Being around arrogant people can be extremely draining, especially for empaths.

Blaming Bens

Blaming Bens love to play the victim. They like to blame all their misfortunes to other people. They do not take responsibility for their actions or their life in general.

Selfish Sam

Selfish Sam's are people who prioritize their self-interest. These people have a little bit of a narcissistic streak. They will do everything just to get what they want.

The Critic

We can all use a constructive criticism every now and then. However, the Critic does not give other feedback to build them up. They just want to rip other people apart so they can feel good about themselves.

Let us take Gina as an example. She used to be a beauty queen, but her good looks have already faded. This made her feel bitter and angry.

Her bitterness pushed her to criticize everyone around her. She would tell her daughter that she is fat even if she is only 125 pounds. She would criticize her staff on a daily basis. She puts people down so she could feel better about herself and her life.

The Ice Queen

Empathy is an important trait because it allows you to fully understand the people around you. It allows you to step into other people's shoes and really feel what they are going through on a daily basis. It helps you build amazing relationships.

Ice queens are cold people who do not have empathy and compassion. They are disrespectful, disinterested, and unresponsive. They make you feel like you are not worthy of their attention and they often minimize your pain, sufferings, and even your needs.

How Negative Energy Directly Affects An Empath?

As mentioned many times in this book, empaths are highly sensitive beings. This means that they feel emotions more intensely than others do. When they are happy, they feel like they are floating in the air. They feel like they are on cloud nine. Every cell in their being exudes joy and excitement.

However, when they are sad, they feel like they are carrying the world on their shoulders. It feels like you are drowning in the sea of sadness and hopelessness. They cannot concentrate.

Empaths experience intense emotional contagion. This means that other people's negative energy affects them strongly.

Let us take Emma and Camille's case as an example. These women work as customer service representatives in a huge telecommunication company. They entertain difficult customers day in and day out.

Camille is a great customer representative. She is empathetic, but she is not an empath. When she talks to a difficult customer, she would sometimes feel bad or angry. However, after the conversation is over, she can easily shake the negative energy off.

Like Camille, Emma is also a great customer service representative. However, she is an empath. Whenever she talks to irate customers, she would feel their stress, anger, and pain. She soon developed depression and anxiety.

Being regularly exposed to negative energy can lead to nightmares, lethargy, and extreme fatigue. It can even lead to suicide ideation. This is why empaths should always try to stay away from toxic people and learn how to block off negative energy.

How to Block Negative Energy and Protect Yourself from Toxic People

Constant exposure to toxic people can lead to a plethora of mental health issues including depression and anxiety.

To protect yourself from toxic people and block negative energy, you have to follow these tips:

Stay away from negative energy.

Distance yourself from toxic people. However, you have to stay at least twenty feet away from an energy vampire.

Create a foolproof plan in dealing with stressful situations.

You must address your empathic needs and honor your sensitivities. Create a plan that you can use in handling emotionally rattling situations.

For example, let us say that you become disoriented and drained whenever your boss questions or belittles your work. You can address this problem in many ways. You can improve the quality of your work to avoid criticism. You can also leave your job and get another one. Alternatively, you can start your own business so you become your own boss.

Creating a solid stress management plan can help you protect your energy and easily handle challenging and draining situations.

Listen to your heart and your gut.

Keep in mind that people are not always, what they seem to be. We live in a world where people wear all sorts of masks. Many people pretend to be someone they are not just to get what they want.

To protect your energy, you must listen to your gut and heart. Be slow to fall into friendship. Before you open yourself up to someone, try to check his/her energy. Stay away if he has/she is giving you bad vibes.

Respect yourself enough to walk away from anything that drains your energy and makes you sad.

Do not take things personally.

One of the best ways to protect yourself from toxic energy is to numb yourself. You have to stop taking things personally. Remember that hurt people hurt other people. Other people's toxic and unhealthy behavior has nothing to do with you.

When you stop taking things personally, you are saving yourself from needless suffering.

Practice guerilla meditation.

Meditation is now one of the biggest buzzwords in the "new age" industry. However, it is more than that.

Meditation is an ancient practice of focusing on a specific word, vision, object, and even person. It has a number of benefits, can strengthen your mind, and help improve your focus.

If you do not have a lot of time for regular meditation practice, you can try guerilla meditation.

This is how you do it: Whenever you feel exposed to an energy vampire, take a step back and close your eyes. Focus your energy on positive experiences. You can think about a goal or a happy memory. You can also think about the things that you are grateful for.

This practice increases your vibrational frequency, blocking negative emotions and energies.

Use healing crystals.

Healing crystals do not only protect you from narcissists. It also protects you from other types of toxic people – the complainers, the manipulators, the pessimists, and the drama queens. We will discuss these stones in the next part of this book.

Set healthy boundaries.

Limit your time with stressful people. If a toxic person asks you to spend a little time with her/him, just say "no". Be clear about what you will and will not tolerate.

Visualize.

Before you leave your house, close your eyes and imagine that you are covered with a protective cloak. This can help you feel secure and protected. Remember that your imagination is powerful. It could instantly raise your vibrational frequency.

Say a powerful mantra.

To avoid getting caught up with someone else's drama, say this mantra "what's yours is yours and what's mine is mine". You can also use the mantra "I do not accept energies that are not mine".

Take the time to be close to nature

Go for a walk. Be close with nature. You do not have to go to the beach or a forest. You can just go to the nearest park and enjoy your local scenic views.

Rub your palms together for 30 seconds to one minute.

Rubbing your palms together creates warmth and friction. This helps switch your moods and ward off negative energy.

Stay away from negativity.

Distance yourself from pessimistic people and surround yourself with people who radiate hope, happiness, and positivity.

Put your foot down.

You have to get clear with people about what you will and will not tolerate. This helps you stay in control of your energy and your life in general. You have to teach other people how to treat you.

Do not react to other people's negativity.

Disarm negative people with a positive response. When someone is putting you down, smile and say "thank you for your opinion" and then walk away.

Do not feed the beast.

Even when you are surrounded with negativity, make a decision to maintain your positivity. The best way to do this is to practice detachment.

Whenever you are feeling down, close your eyes and think about happy memories. Think about your goals. Think about all the things that you are grateful for.

Negativity has no space in your life if you keep feeding yourself with positive thoughts.

Visualize a bubble.

Every morning, close your eyes and focus on your breath. Block out any distracting thoughts and just observe how your chest goes up and down as you breathe.

Concentrate on your breathing. Remove any distracting thought that enters your mind.

Now, imagine that you are in a sacred bubble. This energetic bubble recharges your energetic field, surrounding you with positive energy. This bubble helps you block off negative energy. This bubble helps you remain calm even when someone is freaking out or you are in a highly stressful environment.

Do an aerobic exercise.

Aerobic exercises such as running, walking, dancing, swimming, and cycling help you shake off excess energy. It helps you stay grounded and ward off unwanted energies and emotions.

Lastly, make a daily choice to adopt a positive attitude. Fill your days with joy and gratitude. Always choose to look at the brighter side of things.

Chapter 2 - Practical way of stating the importance of the quirks, behaviors, functions of the mind, and emotions of a sensitive person

Lifestyle Changes for Empaths

Aside from incorporating meditative practices into your daily routine, you can also opt to make lifestyle modifications which can help you maximize your gifts, whilst minimizing the energy draining effects it has on you. Here are a few simple ideas to help you get started:

Start with avoiding people whose energies are toxic to yours. There are those who will purposely manufacture drama in their lives and these are the people you need to stay away from. Try and keep your circle filled with upbeat friends, as well as people who are stable and optimistic.

Another thing you should avoid would be any form of media that affects you adversely. This includes books, unfortunately, as there are certain ones which can trigger ill feelings in many empaths.

It would be god to do a bit of research before purchasing a book or watching a movie this would help you avoid wasting money on something that you won't end up enjoying. Reviews would be very useful for this purpose.

As much as you can, spend plenty of time in nature. Plants are actually great buffers for your emotions and the environment immediately puts you in a more relaxed mood. Treat yourself to getaways a bit more often, even if it's just a quick trip to the country or a garden close to your home.

Do not be afraid of doing things on your own. Most empaths recover better whenever they spend time by themselves. However, not everyone is very comfortable with this solitude. Think about the reason why you're not comfortable and do your best to get better acquainted with this side of you. Your mind will be thanking you for it.

Be more aware of the places you frequent that aren't good for your overall energy. This differs for every empath so a need to be more observant is needed. If you can, avoid these places. Explain to your friends why you cannot stay very long in that area, and suggest other ones that they might enjoy more.

If you explain your needs well enough, they should be able to easily understand the discomfort that being in that environment is giving you.

Be better at handling conflict. Conflict is inevitable chances are, you will never grow to like it. However, you can start managing it better. A counselor would be helpful for this purpose, but if you would rather try and provide a solution to the matter on your own, then there are plenty of self-help books that could give you more insight into it. Just research, you'll find exactly what you need in time.

Most empaths tend to choose professions where they can help other people think teaching, counseling, coaching, and healing. For empaths who are in these particular fields, it is important that you remember self-care.

Learn how to use your energy for yourself. You'll be better at your job too!

Look around your personal space. Is everything organized? Is it clutter-free? A clean environment breeds a clear mind. If you can, always keep your surroundings organized. This lessens the amount of things you need to be anxious about and provides you with a calm place to rest your mind in. Remember, your home must be your sanctuary so treat it as such.

Here's a fact: Despite an empath's efforts to create limits between themselves and energy vampires, there will always be an "emotional hangover" that could happen.

Negative energy tends to linger a lot longer than others, often leaving an empath feeling ill or lacking clarity. In some cases, especially if an empath deals with energy vampires on a daily basis, it would take them a lot of time to recuperate.

So, what can they do in this situation? Well, cleanse themselves of the bad energy is a start. There are many different ways of curing emotional hangovers it really depends on the situation and what the person really needs as well. To help you better understand this and to give you an idea about how to cure emotional hangovers, here are a few strategies to get you started:

Tips for Curing Emotional Hangovers

Shower meditation

If you have enough time during the mornings or during the weekends, use your time in the shower to help cleanse you of any negative energy that might linger. Stay under the shower head and the let water stream from the top of your head all the way to your feet; as this happens, recite the affirmation:

"This water will cleanse all the negative energy from my body, my mind, and my spirit." As you repeat it, visualize that bad energy leaving you. Repeat it until you start feeling lighter. By the end of it, you will feel a lot more rejuvenated.

In continuing with cleansing and adjusting your space to meet your needs, try using salt lamps as well as negative ion generators. What these would do is produce negative ions which then clears the environment of different pollutants such as mold spores, dust, pollen, odors, viruses, cigarette smoke and different types of bacteria.

Light a white-colored candle.

This is especially useful when you're meditation or simply unwinding after a long day. This creates a calming mood and also helps in removing negativity your surroundings.

Aromatherapy

Take advantage of the soothing effects that aromatherapy has. Rosewater is a favorite among many people, but choose the scent you feel most comfortable with. You can use sprays or synthetic oils which you'll need to add to diffusers in order to spread the aroma around. You can even choose purifying scents such as frankincense, myrrh and sage.

Nature

We've already established how effective being in nature can be if you want to ground yourself. Grounding takes this one step further and actually connects you to the ground first, take your shoes off and stand barefoot on the ground. Do this while your practice both visual and breathing meditation.

You'll find that focusing on nothing but the sound of your breath really helps clear the mind of any negative thoughts. The earth, with its own natural energy, will replenish yours the longer you stay grounded to it.

Create your sanctuary.

If you live with other people, it is important to create a safe space for yourself. You'll need this if you want to properly meditate and keep any distractions at bay. It need not be an entire room. In fact, even a corner of your bedroom would work just as fine as long as it has the basics: incense, candles, flowers, and a totem that you can focus your gaze on while you meditate.

Now, when should you practice some of these tips? There need not be a "time" for it. These are basically small lifestyle changes you can add to your everyday life. Things that you can turn to whenever the emotional hangover becomes a little too burdensome for you.

As an empath, you'll find that this will happen a lot. So, instead of only acting when the problem arises, always be one step ahead and prepare for the situation.

Chapter 3 - Highly sensitive introverts 'strengths and struggles.

Empaths have a great deal of strengths that support them in living complete, wonderful lives. When you begin to come to terms with your identity as an Empath and you integrate protection and self-care measures into your life, working in alignment with your empathic gift will become easier. This means that you can begin to enjoy the many benefits and strengths of being an Empath.

Here are some of the wonderful strengths you can look forward to developing and embodying when you awaken to your empathic abilities and begin to take control over them:

A Great Power

Empaths are extremely powerful. This is one of the reasons society puts them down so much. They are afraid of their power. As an individual who can sense things about people that they may not be willing to share, or who can deeply connect to plants and animals around them, you possess clear differences from the average person. In modern society, there are a lot of individuals who are deeply disconnected from the world around them. They struggle to tune in on basic levels, never mind as deeply as you do. You may see it as a weakness, but that is only because you have been conditioned to. In reality, you possess a great power. Once you learn to embrace it and use it to your advantage, you will be unstoppable in creating positive change in the world.

An Amazing Friend

Anyone who has an Empath as a friend should be incredibly grateful. Empaths are amazing friends. Empaths truly cherish the people they love in their life and will go to extreme lengths to help and protect them. They give great advice to their friends. When a friend has a problem or some sort of difficulty, Empaths are happy to use their beautiful gift of empathizing and putting themselves in their friend's shoes to understand the particular situation and figure out what the best possible decision is.

Ability to Detect Red Flags

Because of your ability to see what is going on beneath the surface, you have an uncanny ability to detect red flags in any person or situation. You do this by empathizing with the other person, essentially allowing you to step into their shoes. This means that you can detect the harmony between the person's words, actions and feelings. There, you can determine whether they are acting in alignment with the truth or if they are lying or being dishonest in any way. By sensing any signs of incongruence, you are able to detect possible ulterior motives. Whether or not you choose to actually recognize and act on these is a completely different story, but your ability to detect them and become aware of them is extremely powerful. You are capable of knowing any time there is something inherently wrong about a situation, making it easy for you to avoid danger and energetic attacks if you are tuned in and capable of acting on this information. If you are not yet, do not worry. As an Empath, you are capable of tapping into this ability at any time. It is not too late for you.

Detecting Compulsive Liars

Another great ability you have with being able to tell what is truly going on under the surface of others is that you can easily detect compulsive liars. When people are lying, you know it almost instantly. Just like the red flags, you can detect the harmony between the person's words, actions and feelings. By recognizing any signs of disharmony, it can be easy for you to suspect lying. This often comes as just a "knowingness" within. This encourages you to refrain from believing them and can support you in preventing yourself from getting drawn in and trapped in their web of lies. The more you practice this, the better you will become at using this gift.

If you are a wounded healer and not able to utilize your gift efficiently, you may find yourself getting trapped into a person's web of lies. This is something important to address in the process of healing this archetype, if you have it.

Strong Creative Talents

Individuals who are gifted Empaths are known to be very strong in their creative talents. As we have already discussed, they are skilled artists, singers, poets, writers and creators in general. Empaths view the world in a poetic way that enables them to create unique art pieces that highlight their unique view on the world. Their ability to visualize something in their head and bring it into the material world with their creativity is simply amazing. The challenge for most Empaths is first eliminating all the negativity they have absorbed growing up. This negativity could be in the form of doubt, insecurity, fear of failure, and lack of confidence.

Virtually every Empath has the potential to be creative, though how they express or use the trait may vary. In other words, not every Empath will be great at the same thing, but they all will have some degree of creativity that they can use to express themselves and serve the world. This is incredibly satisfying and fulfilling for the Empath.

Excellent Problem Solvers

When an Empath has developed their empathic gift, they can be excellent problem solvers. Using their empathetic ability, they are able to analyze the wants and needs of different parties from multiple points of view. By being able to analyze a certain situation and see many different points of view, gives the Empath a great edge to be able to come up with the best possible solution that will be beneficial for both parties.

Great Entrepreneurship Abilities

Because of their intuitive abilities and their superb ability to solve problems, Empaths make great entrepreneurs. They are highly focused on delivering the best results to their clients, no matter what their line of work may be. Furthermore, they are heavily driven by a desire to have freedom and to escape from the toxic, overwhelming, and greedy environments of traditional 9 - 5 jobs.

Empath entrepreneurs are great at coming up with creative companies that reach the needs of their clients in ways that larger companies tend to overlook completely. They typically find themselves in their own companies that offer some form of healing or shifting modern society. Counselors, life and business coaches, alternative healers, artists, writers, and other career paths are extremely common for Empaths to choose.

Fortunately, each of these can be done on an entrepreneurial basis. They are also excellent choices as they cater to the unique strengths and weaknesses of the Empath, allowing them to shine their brightest and serve in the way that their soul needs to shine.

If you are an Empath and you are not presently on the path of being an entrepreneur, you may find great joy and benefit in beginning this life path. With your gifts and abilities, you have the capacity to begin your life as an entrepreneur and create great success in doing so. There are many great benefits to choosing this career path. Some of these benefits include:

You are able to experience much more flexibility and freedom in your life compared to working a job

You can control your own working schedule and holidays

You do not have to deal with the draining and toxic environments of a 9-5 job

You can choose the people you want to work with or work solely online

You can work from home

You have the potential to earn much more than what a job can offer you

You can put your creative ability to good use

Become more fulfilled and happy in what you do

More travel opportunities may present themselves to you

General health and happiness will improve when you remove yourself from negative, toxic work environments

Many people believe that empathic entrepreneurship is the way of the future. As more and more people seek to lead a more socially conscious and responsible life, many are avoiding large businesses and corporations that are typically known for being irresponsible, unkind, and savage in their business dealings. These exact same people are seeking entrepreneurs running their own socially responsible businesses in a way that genuinely serves their needs on a personal level. As an Empath, you have exactly what it takes to serve in this way, meaning that you and your gifts are exactly what these people are looking for.

Strong Relation to Animals and Plants

Another great strength possessed by Empaths is their connection to animals and plants. As you know from animal Empaths and plant Empaths, these individuals have incredible talents when it comes to communicating with animals and plants. This is a breath of fresh air in a world where very little concern has been shown to the environment and those who inhabit it. Many humans in the modern world rarely consider other humans, let alone other species or life forms. As an Empath, you may have a powerful ability to relate to these life forms and protect them from the destruction of humans who experience little to no empathy in their lives.

Animals and plants are also believed to be Empathic, meaning that you may find that animals and plants respond well to you, also. You may find yourself attracting animals into your life and having an uncanny ability to help plants thrive in a way that others may struggle to do. This is because they are intuitive and can sense that you are kind. This allows them to automatically trust in you and feel safe, protected and nourished in your presence. They sense your energy, and it supports them in thriving.

Chapter 4 - How to reduce fears and insecurities through experiences in the real world.

Are you afraid of being in a large group of people? Do you feel anxious when you are about to meet new people?

Understanding the Problem

If this is the case, you need to find out why. You also need to identify the specific aspects of being in a crowd and meeting new people that make you anxious. There is a pattern on how the fear or anxiety builds up. For most people, it starts with a trigger. Your fear may start when you hear that you need to attend the social events. Some introverts only hate social events when they did not expect it. Others become fearful when they need to take part in a social activity that focuses attention to them. This fear is usually related to performance in the social setting.

Fear is normal. It is a natural way for our body to warn us of danger. However, it can be socially debilitating, especially if fear creates a habit of preventing us from doing our duties.

Let's take Mike for example. Mike is about to spend his 3rd Christmas in the company. He did not attend the two first Christmas parties of the company because there are always activities where he can get embarrassed. He tries to talk himself into going to the activity but his fear always wins. In the past two years, he always decides, on the last minute, to stay home and make up some excuse on why he can't make it.

In the past two holiday parties, Mike did not understand why he does not want to go. However, as he analyzed the pattern of fear, he realized that it was performing in the crowd that made him anxious. He enjoyed the idea of having a good time with his colleagues and he even looks forward to talking to some of the people. However, whenever the idea of performing in front of his coworkers pops in his mind, he begins to feel anxious. He starts imagining scenarios wherein he becomes embarrassed.

By knowing the specific part of the party that Mike fears, he may be able to avoid the performance part instead of avoiding the whole event altogether.

Triggers are thoughts of social activities that start the fear in your mind. When the fear starts, a socially anxious person begins a series of activities that will lead him to avoid certain social activities. In the professional world, missing certain events and activities may be interpreted as not being a team player.

To prevent your social fear from stopping you from doing something, you need to identify the specific cause of your fear. Here are some of the common social activities that people fear:

• Speaking in public

• Doing something while a huge crowd is watching

• Being teased or laughed at

• Presenting in front of people with authority

• Being on a date or meeting someone you are romantically interested in

• Giving a performance on stage

• Starting a casual conversation

In most cases, most people realize that the things they fear the most are not important and that they can actually fight it. However, some introverts never find the willpower to fight their fears even when they know that the scenario they fear may not actually happen. Here are some of the things that you can do to prevent your fear from taking over your actions:

Control How you Think to Deal with your Fears.

There are certain thinking patterns that socially anxious individuals often use. Here are some of them:

• Assumptions and predictions

People who are anxious assume that there are always opportunities in events for them to become embarrassed. They make a lot of assumptions that lead to their fears. They also make predictions on how things will happen. For people with social anxiety, this becomes a habit.

When you begin assuming and predicting fearful scenarios, it is a signal that you need to distract your mind from the fear. People have different coping mechanisms against fear. If you are in the office when the fear happens for example, you can occupy your mind with work to prevent it from ruling over your thoughts.

• Extreme negative thinking

The assumptions and predictions of introverts who have social anxiety are usually worsened by their extreme negativity. When thinking of these events, they focus on the worst things that may happen.

• Personalizing

When thinking of the things that can go wrong in the social events, they also focus on how the people in the party will react towards them. They think that people are out to make fun of them. They imagine that the bosses are there to humiliate them.

• The flight or fight response

When the fear starts, stress hormones will then activate their flight or fight response. For socially anxious introverts, the automatic response is to avoid the event. They may have made the choice not to attend the event in the past and they turned out all right. Whenever they faced the same type of stress after that, they decided to use the same response to the stress.

Over time, these patterns of thinking become automatic when they are required to attend events that they are not familiar with. Continued use of these patterns of thinking and behavior prevents a person from enjoying social success.

How to Prevent Social Fears?

Breathing exercises

Breathing is one of the few functions that our body performs with both the conscious and subconscious mind. Being able to control the subconscious acts of breathing by being conscious of them is a powerful tool. One of the first signs of anxiety is an increased pace of shallow breaths. This may happen when you are about to go to the event. It may also happen even when thinking of the event. When you feel this happening, you should try to take back your control of your breathing. For example, when you feel that you are becoming nervous or fearful about a certain social situation, you should find a chair and do the following breathing exercise:

1. Sit and relax on the chair with your back straight and your face forward. Put your right hand on your right lap and your left hand on the surface of your stomach.

2. Slowly take a deep breath through your nose while expanding your stomach as the air comes in. Take at least 4 seconds to inhale. Hold the air in for 2 seconds before you slowly exhale it. Exhale through your mouth. It should take more than 4 seconds for you to exhale all the air out.

3. You should do this for 2 minutes or until you feel relaxed. By the time you are done, any fast-paced shallow breathing should be gone.

Change anxiety-related behavior with actions related to countering your fear

For most people, the flight response becomes a habit after the trigger. In the beginning, a socially anxious introvert may still try to convince himself to go to the event. Over time, the person no longer considers going. Every time an idea of attending an event makes him feel uncomfortable, he automatically decides not to go.

You can change such habit even if you have been practicing it for years. All you have to do is to identify the trigger of your fear and explain in detail the behavior that follows it. You should then identify the rewarding feeling that you get when you decide not to attend an event because of fear.

Now that you have identified that cycle of your habit, you need to associate bad feelings towards the habit. Think of the negative effects of the habit. Make a list of it so that you can remind yourself of the negative effects that the habit has done for you. This will convince your subconscious mind that the habit is not doing any good for you.

Next, you need to think of a behavior change in response to the trigger. As mentioned above, first comes the trigger. It is then followed by the routine of the habit. The trigger feeling and the fear will always be there. You cannot change that. You can change the behavior that follows the fear. Let's say you always avoid your family holiday dinners because of some embarrassing experience. Every time you think of the event, you feel embarrassed inside. Over time, this feeling has developed into fear that the same experience will happen in the future.

You need to decide to go. You must not argue with yourself or waiver between the decision of going or not. When you have decided that you will go to the next one, your next challenge will be the thoughts that will bring back memories of your dreaded embarrassing experience. To prevent it from affecting your decision, you should look for a way to change your behavior every time memories of the experiences enter your mind.

Instead of thinking too much about it, you can say the phrase "I'm going" and think of another thought. Every time your fear of social events creeps in, you should say this phrase. Verbalizing it creates a sense of strength in most people. It symbolizes the change in habit that will bring them back to attending social events for good.

Lastly, you should identify the trigger as it happens. Every time you feel the fear, start anticipating the behavior that follows. You should then use the phrase used above or any variation of it to prevent your mind from going into the habit.

Expose your mind to your fear

One of the best ways to deal with fear is to face it. You may feel overwhelmed if you face all of your fears all at once. A better strategy is to face them one at a time. Instead of going to all the social events that you are invited to, you should focus your mind to only one. Once you have attended that event, you should think of the next one that you will attend. You should assure yourself that the worse case scenario that you think up in your head is always your irrational fear speaking and will probably not happen.

After attending dozens of social events, you will begin to enjoy the experience. You will start to develop courage when you fear something about an event. As you go to more events, the habit of going to them begins to develop. Once that habit develops that's when the magic happens and your confidence take a noticeable turn for the best. The key is changing your habits.

Chapter 5 - How to find potential friends

People dislike being lonely, and if they sense that they can feel less alone by engaging another person in a simple conversation, then they will. A lot of shy people tend to feel alone because they cannot find the courage to talk to another person, even if they are sharing the same space. However, there are certain social conventions that might be the cause of anxiety, conventions that prompt one to think that it is difficult to deal with other people and that one is much safer without inviting a new person into one's life. After all, most shy people have been let down by others at some point, and it is an act of self-preservation to be anxious around strangers.

Strangers

Solitude can be unhealthy for some, and it can even make one feel that he or she is unprepared for "battle." When shy kids enter school, for example, they are forced into social interaction at a level that is unprecedented for most children at that age, making them engage in a battle armed with a gun, but no bullets. Some children can become cynically shy. In other words, they may feel so disconnected from the rest of the world that they become hostile towards others. In a world where everybody seems to want to make connections, being left out can be utterly frustrating. A lot of shy people do try to connect with those around them, contrary to the belief that shyness is equivalent to passiveness. Those who are shy are excited to be invited to events, but they often feel depressed due to their perception that their preparation is incomplete, since after all, they cannot muster the courage to start a conversation. Some seek the courage to connect through lowering their inhibitions with alcohol and drugs, a solution that is temporary at best, not to mention potentially fatal.

People are encouraged to talk to others in order to prevent feelings of hate and animosity towards others who belong in social groups. At the end of the day, everyone wants to feel belongingness and acceptance, as well as to feel that the world is a safe place.

friends

Once you make it past the introductions and the first few generic conversational lines, you must find a way to distinguish yourself from others who might, at first glance, seem rather similar.

If your newfound potential friends never learn anything distinctive about you, due either to your own shyness or to conversations simply never getting passed the most mundane of topics, it is unlikely that you will ever develop a deeper connection with them. There would simply be no way for them to know if the two of you have anything in common worth pursuing, any shared interests that you may want to delve into a deeper conversation about one day. They will be unaware of your strengths, your weaknesses, your quirks and your charms. Of course, this is hardly information you need to display openly to anyone and some traits might very well be best kept firmly under wraps until true intimacy is established but revealing select tidbits that might prove interesting can allow you to build and enhance new friendships by opening up about yourself. In turn, your new companions will be more inclined to do the same, possibly revealing shared eccentricities, interests or lifestyle choices that you can enjoy and/or discuss together in more detail.

Often, the biggest detriment to letting others see glimpses of our personality and interests is due to shame. What if they dislike those features or interests, and we simply embarrass ourselves? What if they consider the information we share out of place or too forward and everything is awkward between them and us forever? All too often we convince ourselves that the things we like and our own personalities will not be liked by others, but the only way to know is to let prospective friends know about these things. If you hide them, you will be rather bland since none of your best personality features or fun interests will be shown at all. You will also eliminate the chance of learning if they might enjoy similar pastimes or share your quirks and that would be a shame because shared interests and features are a surefire way to trigger bonding and a memorable impression.

As for technique on how to accomplish this, it is actually fairly straightforward. If something comes up that interests or excites you, simply mention it. Ask your acquaintance their thoughts on it and share yours. In this way, you can discuss skills, hobbies, even qualities you possess or value in others in a relatively organic way. Be careful not to force your viewpoints upon your chat companion. Express yourself in an enthusiastic but non-judgmental manner. You might discover that you have a lot in common, but the reverse could also happen. Even if you discover that you have little in common with the person who was so recently a stranger, it will do you little good to burn bridges or create an enemy. If you discover that your opinions diverge in a manner too significant to move past pleasantly, change the topic or if you must, politely end the conversation. If on occasion someone does hold different values or simply does not seem to share any of your interests, do not take it personally. In many cases, if you approach such people with flexibility and genuine interest, you might find that you have more in common than you thought or at the very least you will gain an interesting new perspective. Ultimately, no harm is likely to befall you from making your own interests and personality traits apparent, the worst case scenario, you simply both move on, leaving your own mentalities firmly intact. In other scenarios, you may be able to enjoy conversing with even someone with very different viewpoints from your own once you understand the reasoning behind them. Do not let fears of shame, judgment or rejection keep you from letting others see who you really are. It is the only way you can have valid and legitimate conversations with others, and that is worth the relatively minor risk incurred.

Colleagues

When running into a long-lost friend, colleague, or acquaintance, you can be more informal. Even a simple, "Hello! How are you? It's been a long time" will start the conversation, perhaps even lead to a longer conversation or a future hookup. Still, it doesn't hurt to know these tips to ensure that an accidental meeting can become productive and pleasant.

☐ Show your enthusiasm for the meeting. You can say, "It's been forever! How are you?" or "I haven't seen you for so long! What's up?"

☐ Smile and make eye contact, too. You may either shake hands or hug each other depending on your past relationship, although a physical touch isn't mandatory in all cases.

☐ Listen to the information shared by your friend and offer your own personal information, too. But keep it brief since there's little need to go into the gory details of your life. Ask about other members of the family, if you're familiar with them, too, since it shows your concern and extends the conversation.

You don't have to share details if you aren't comfortable with it. Just say, "Oh, nothing special, just the usual work-study-home routine" or "Same old, same old." You may, nonetheless, have to offer just a little bit more if the other person graciously offered a tidbit of information about what's up with his/her life.

End the small talk with an invitation to spend time in the future, which may or may not be definite. You can say, "Let's get together for coffee sometime," but you don't necessarily have to ask for the other person's contact details or give yours unless you're being asked for it. You can give your social media account, or your cellphone number, or your email address, whichever suits your mood at the moment.

Chapter 6 - Introversion, Shyness, and Love

Being introverted is more of a personal characteristic that is based on inner emotions rather than focusing on outer stimuli. Being an introvert does not make you fretful and shy. On the contrary, introverts are quiet but bold as a lion. They are not easily tossed around by others because most of the time, they are stern and smart – they know what they want and would stop at nothing to get it. To be shy is to be afraid of people and the situation at hand. One's inability to deliver a composed speech at a social or official gathering due to shyness isn't an indication that such a fellow is an introvert; it is a sign of fear. Although introverted people typically do not like moving close to others, they do appreciate it when they are around intimate people.

Quite a handful of people have mistaken shyness for introversion and have received the most shocking surprise ever. Some extroverts wish to have an introvert as a spouse. Because they cannot differentiate between introversion and shyness, they are caught in the middle. Most of them ended up getting the extroverted, shy partner or the ones with the personality that is neither introverted nor extroverted. These are the ones we earlier discussed to fall between the line.

Kayla was an easy-going, beautiful woman. One day, she was trying to get a shower after the day's work when she heard her next-door neighbor screaming at the top of her voice. It was a hotel room, so, she had every right to ignore the noise and mind her business. She went to the hotel every time she had business to settle out of town. This was one of her trips, and she had worked all day. Nothing was more important to her than her rest and a quiet environment at the moment. She had always chosen that particular hotel for its serenity over a period of time.; but that day made her want to regret her choice of hotel. She just needed a sound sleep and then this brouhaha. When the chattering wouldn't stop, she angrily left her room to find out what the problem was. On getting to the entrance of the door, she overheard the lady screaming, "How dare you treat me like trash? You don't care about anyone but you" and the ranting continued. Kayla had no choice but to knock. No way was she going to have a sound sleep with this woman been left alone. The door was opened, and she got in. After all said and done, Kayla discovered that Nora had misjudged Steeve. She thought he was just been shy when they met when in actual sense, Steeve was an introvert. He liked been left alone. He was not the outgoing type and didn't seem to be interested in things that caught Nora's fancy. Nora thought Steeve might be having an affair. Steeve on the other hand, when asked why he chose to shut Nora out of his world, replied by saying "I thought she was like me." Steeve had mistaken Nora's shyness for introversion on their first meeting. It wasn't too long that he found out that she was directly opposite of him. Nora always wanted to go shopping, hang around with friends, and get Steeve to talk about everything!

Kayla who was an introvert like Steeve had to seat Nora down and advised she either work on making the relationship work by accepting Steeve for who he truly was or just quit and walk away. For the first time in hours, there was peace in the vicinity.

From the story above, we see how most people mistake shyness for introversion. Although Steeve and Nora have been living peacefully with each other by learning to respect each other's personality, Nora must have gone through a lot to bring serenity into her home. When asked how she managed the saga, she said "to fall and stay in love with an introvert you must understand the following;"

1. Don't demand too much.

Introverts do not like it when people ask for too much of them. They don't want to be that seat filler that fills every empty seat in your life. He loves to be a part of your life but not you choking him with too much of you.

2. Don't be in haste.

Due to his quiet nature, an introvert would always like to take things slow, be it physically or emotionally. Rushing things up might piss him off and send him off.

3. Be original.

Introverted people are thrilled when they meet people who are original. He has enough in his head to analyze, do not add to the list with a bogus life.

4. Love silence

Sometimes, the introverts do not want to talk or be talked to. All he wants is to enjoy silence. Do not try to break that chain of fun. Respect his choice and pull back by giving him the space he needs.

5. Grow listening ears.

Introverts are though quiet people, but sometimes they want to talk too. They want to have that assurance that someone cares enough to hear them out.

6. Be sincere.

Nothing thrills an introvert more than other people's sincerity. Introverts understand how difficult it is to have people who can be trusted. People who say things the way they are without mincing words. Once you are tested and trusted, you can get them to open up to you at a cost next to nothing.

Chapter 7 Result-oriented ways of Improving Self-Esteem and Self-Confidence

As earlier illustrated in the book, we were opened up to the importance of ideal self-esteem and self-confidence in one's life. Likewise, we can practically see that the two factors can determine the level of achievement. That is why this section will be unveiling various ways you can enhance your self-esteem as well as your self-confidence. Also, due to the close similarity between these two factors, the enhancement option below will work in boosting both factors.

Here we go:

Have the "Can do" Spirit: Exhibiting the "can do' spirit is an essential quality in every trace blazer. It simply means you should believe in yourself about achieving specific things. According to the common saying, if you don't help yourself, nobody can help you". This doesn't literarily mean no one will try to help you in some ways; they would. But the desired change still lies with the action you will take personally. Quite a lot of successful people out there have faced various hurdles to get to the point they are now. And what makes them different is their capacity to infuse themselves with the 'Can do' mentality, assuring themselves that no matter what the constraints ahead of them may be, they will face it and actualize their goal.

Build capacity (Self-development): Unpreparedness has also been found as a significant cause of low self-esteem and self-confidence. In light of this, you should ensure grooming yourself in any way possible. Are you going for a presentation, exam, tutoring, or deliberation? Equipping yourself with relevant information ahead of time will undoubtedly enhance your confidence and self-esteem beyond your expectations.

Know your strengths and weakness: A mistake some people do commit is by thinking every trace blazer out there is perfect in all ways. Unlike what you might be thinking, those world shakers also have their weaknesses deeply buried in them. But what they are doing different is realizing and leveraging their strengths to stand out of the crowd. This is why it becomes vital to take a moment, think deep in identifying your strength, then work around it to make the difference you desire. Nonetheless, no weakness can't be worked upon; aside from leveraging your strength, attending to your weakness to convert it to advantage will go a long way in boosting your self-esteem and confidence.

Discard negative thoughts from your mind: If care is not taken, negative thoughts can make you fail where you have 100% capacity to win. Negativity is also a major player in reducing one's self-esteem and confidence; however, you have the key to make its power have no effect on your life. And the key is countering the thoughts with positive thoughts.

Think about your achievements: There are specific situations or moments in life where we tend to feel intimidated, querying our inner consciousness, or challenge the belief that we are ever capable of overcoming a hurdle. At this point, if one is not careful, the rush of negative thoughts through your mind might adversely affect one's confidence as well as self-esteem. But a quick and alternative cause of action needed in eliminating the adverse is by thinking about the achievement you have also bagged in the past. What this does is to encourage you that if you achieve a specific goal in the past, you are definitely capable of overcoming the challenge ahead of you.

Go slow on your communication with others: Some people may think that the need to talk a bit slower will not in any way boost one's self-esteem and confidence. The fact is that how you present your conversation greatly determines the level of accolade you attract from your audience. For some, they have the in-depth knowledge of what they are talking about, but talking too fast as the thought rushes through their brain might prevent them from clearly illustrating their point; this might decrease their confidence and esteem, probably for not being able to meet expectation on the discussion or presentation. But don't you think going slow and steady in rolling your speeches out will make your audience want to listen to you more?

So, if you are the type that experience some difficulties when passing verbal information across to others, it will do you a great deal of good to take it slowly. This will boost people's eagerness to listen to what you have to say, and this, in turn, will boost your morale for a more excellent experience. Therefore, you must understand that presenting your thought slowly doesn't make you less capable of having the right impact on your audience.

Facing a challenge is a must for successful people

Many people out there still believe challenges must be avoided at all cost. Do you fall among this category of people? The fact here is that, without challenges in life, we will remain in the same spot and our situation can further get worse. Challenge is that hurdle one must successfully scale through to experience not only the next phase of life but greater height. Imagine someone that doesn't want to sit for promotional exam due to the fear of failing. Imagine an individual that doesn't want to work but desires to earn sustainable income. What of an athlete that always dreams of winning without wanting to go through the challenges of rigorous training? The simple ideology here is that challenges are steps to greater height. And aside from scaling to them, your self-esteem and confidence are also developing, with the capacity to handle subsequent challenges.

Aside from the above hints to improving your self-esteem and confidence, the followings will also come in handy and should also be added to your rule of engagement:

consider change as a constant factor in life, and always be ready for it.

strive to create solutions to peoples' needs around you.

always exhibiting friendly gestures like smiling, responding to greeting among others.

appreciate the people around you.

keep yourself physically fit.

manage your time well.

avoid idleness

take small strides toward your desired goals; slow and steady have the potential of winning the race.

don't procrastinate.

Knowledge gives access to power. With all the above-listed arsenal in your weaponry, it becomes vital to add one more thing, and that is discipline. This makes you stick to your plan irrespective of the situation. Lastly, never forget to keep yourself motivated!

Chapter 8 - Introvert People and Relationships

Difficulties, Practical Tips to Improve your Relationships (With Friends and Your Partner for Men and Women)

This situation then means that the introvert may be compelled to move out of their comfort zones so that they maintain the relationships that they have formed and that they value.

The thing with introverts is that, for the most part, they will often form relationships that they want to establish. The people that they keep around, the people that they hang around are usually people that the introvert wants to have around.

Now, as with any relationship out there, you will come across relationship problems as an introvert. In your case, though, your introversion makes things a little more complicated. For example;

Differing Communications Styles

How many times have you and the people in your life fought? If we are honest, it is a couple of times, if it's a healthy relationship.

Now, when you look at things from your perspective, you often take the time just after a bit of confrontation to get lost in your thoughts momentarily. Because of this, the person in your life may come to take this as a sign that you are avoiding them when in reality, you are accepting the time, as you are wont to do, to comb through your thoughts.

Extroverts often find that they are more responsive in a fast-paced scenario. If you are an introvert and you begin dating an extrovert, the different ways that you communicate could create some friction between the two of you.

Communication is an integral part of a healthy relationship. Therefore, as an introvert, your desire to be in your own world and make worlds out of your own thoughts will often mean that you will place little value and emphasis on the real-world relationships that you have, leading to a nasty breakdown in communication, which is only the first step in a decreasing value of the connection.

As stated, a few introverts may also suffer from shyness, which would then mean that they will have an even harder time communicating effectively due to their low confidence and social anxiety. This situation can crumble the relationship.

Being Quiet Can be Read Wrong in A Conflict

How many events of conflict have you found yourself in? Probably more than a few times, right?

The thing is that, because of their quiet and calm demeanor, introverts will often not display their full range of emotions. When they are angry, they will often talk will composure, and when things indeed do get to a head, rather than explode (unless really pushed), an introvert will sit back quietly and ruminate. You have done it, right?

Now, many people out here are extroverts. They understand that conflict is an exchange that has both people going at each other. However, in your case, your silence and calmness can be looked at as a lack of concern or as a show that you do not value what the other person is saying. If you are at work and it is your boss confronting you, you may inexplicably be giving off the vibe that you do not take what they are saying seriously.

If you disagree with your significant other, you may come off as being arrogant towards them, as uncaring, even when this is not true. When you do not take care, this situation can lead to a breakdown in communication, which could adversely affect your relationships, which means so much to you.

Conflicting Needs with Your Partner/Friends

When you date someone o is more outgoing, the chances are that your personalities may overlap and cross paths.

So, there you are, having gotten used to spending your quality time alone, curled up on a sofa with a book perhaps, or a movie. Then you get into a relationship and suddenly, you need to make plans to go out with your partner.

While these kinds of differences can be ironed out with communication, there is still often that feeling of dissatisfaction when you push yourself to get out more and become more outgoing, which can result in frequent problems between you and your spouse.

When you and your partner go out, and they need to take a picture, you will have to do it, even when you are uncomfortable with it. These kinds of situations always arise and may lead to conflicts.

You Don't Like Talking About Yourself.

Imagine yourself going out on a first date. Wow! Butterflies and all! But then you get there, and immediately you realize that you may not be too keen to talk about yourself to this new person. Even after a few dates, you may still not be comfortable.

This desire to not reveal too much about themselves will often cost many introverts relationships.

To build relationships requires that we become comfortable in being vulnerable with the other person. This helps foster trust and allows people to bond more deeply.

While an introvert will cherish the chance to form deep bonds with others, the thing is that they will often do that in the hopes that they do not get to reveal too much about themselves. It is usually not because they have something to hide. Perhaps it is because they may feel overwhelmed then or probably may not be too deep in the relationship yet. Introverts take their time to build relationships, which then, can make a frustrating experience for the extroverted friend or partner.

Because of your lack of desire to talk about yourself, you may then come off as disinterested, and perhaps the partner may interpret this as a sign that you do not value them.

Over-Thinking

Hey, thinking is great! You sure do know that. But then, as with anything else, it can become problematic when overdone.

The natural tendency of an introvert to become obsessed with details and planning and observing and decoding will often mean that they approach almost everything from a thinker's perspective.

In shopping, you obsess over the choices you are to make. The jam is too sugary, but the marmalade that you want has run out. The alternative jelly looks good, but it is from a brand you don't know, but the third option looks promising. The fourth option appears like a cheap knock-off of your fave. The fifth option is far down, and so on.

This issue can be frustrating to the people that are in your life. Because of your desire to make the right decision, your obsession with details might create a wedge between you and the people around you.

In this case, this scenario could lead to your friends and partners avoiding you as you begin to become dull.

While it may appear superficial and vain, overthinking may be counterproductive in the long-term as this will mean that you get caught in the paradox of choice, and you may end up choosing the worse option.

You Struggle in A Group Setting

As we have stated, as an introvert, you find great solace in your own company. In that alone time, that is often most of the time, you brainstorm ideas, create stories and drawn art. You toy around with thoughts and ideas and concepts. Essentially, you become your biggest library.

But then, when you go out with your friends, you find yourself as part of a group. Suddenly, doors close shut in your mind. The stories you wanted to tell are locked inside. With all the people around, the interactions drain all your energy. Unable to access your inner thoughts, you become quiet in the group, and you come off as just a hanger-on. Your friends begin to think that you do not value the relationship, even when you reassure them that you do. Your actions seem not to match your words.

Being an introvert means that it is hard to survive in situations that acknowledges extroversion.

What this does then is, it can create friction between you and your friends. You will appear stuck-up and unwilling to take part in the interactions, even though the truth is that you are not really able to access your best thoughts in a group setting. This is also frustrating to you as an introvert too. You can't adequately explain why you do not know how to think well when with others. As such, it becomes hard to create a connection with others.

If it is in your romantic relationship when your partner begins to take note that you enjoy being on your own, perhaps more than you enjoy being with them, they will distance themselves too, in the knowledge that you do not need them.

So, to avoid these scenarios, what could be the solutions?

Ways to Build Better Relationships as an Introvert

Embrace Yourself

Because of the cynical view that people attach to the introvert, it might be easy then for some introverts to go to extreme lengths to create a fake extroverted exterior so that they can obtain other people's approval.

The obvious thing here is that you are already setting up the relationship for failure by pretending to be someone you are not, which is dishonesty. Aside from this, though, you will be unable to communicate well how you feel about things and thus, will be forced to double down so that you do not sell yourself out. This occurrence goes on and on until it gets to a point where you can't take it any longer, and you snap. Things change suddenly, and now, your relationships stand on the brink of collapse, balancing precariously on the edge of a precipice

You can avoid this. To build better relationships, many relationship experts will advise that you first begin by loving yourself. As an introvert, this will mean coming to terms with your introversion and understanding how you communicate and how you want others to communicate with you. What is your love language? How do you show your displeasure? What words of affirmation do you use, and which ones do you appreciate when someone tells you? How do you like to be touched? What gestures do you want? Gifts? Words?

Only through becoming comfortable with yourself will you then be able to move on to the other steps.

Use Your Knack for Listening to Your Advantage

This skill is one of your key strengths as an introvert. As such, it can be a powerful tool to use to create a better rapport with the people that you come into contact with or interact with.

But now, to build from this, rather than just listening, take time after the other person is done talking to say back what they have said to you. This active strategy will allow you to gauge how well you listen while also letting the other person know that someone is listening to them. People often will feel closer to other people that make them feel worthy. By repeating back what the other person has said (not in the exact words obviously) you tell them indirectly that you value them and want to interact more with them. You will find that you will create better relationships without having to pretend to be outgoing or loud.

Also, listen to learn about the other person. You will be amazed at how this will quickly allow you to bond with them.

Accept Invitations to Parties Sometimes

Yes, I know this freaks you out, but social circles are often built and maintained by frequent time spent together. When you have friends, and they make the point to include you to events, you could work with them in how you will accept the invitations.

To create strong bonds with them, being honest with them will create a situation where they can extend an invitation to you, and you can accept some and reject others, or maybe even accept all of them but them come to an agreement with them that you leave early.

We all thrive on social bonds, so don't isolate yourself too much. Say yes to going out sometimes, but of course, not at the expense of your mental state. Your friends should be able to respect the boundaries that you agree on, and you do the same.

Be Kind to Strangers

Well, mainly we should be kind to everyone. But, for the most part, many people are often rude to strangers when it is undeserved. Because of this, it is in many of us a habit to treat strangers with indifference and disdain in some instances.

As an introvert trying to build better relationships, try by being the opposite - be kind to strangers. What this does is that it helps you acknowledge the humanity of the other person. by being thankful to the cashier, you begin to tell them that they matter. By pardoning the person that stepped on your toes, you tell them that you acknowledge that to err is human.

When you are with your friends, this will help them feel more connected to you and want to associate with you. You will win their admiration, and they will most likely want to associate more with you.

On the other hand, you will create a vast pool of potential friends with the people that you are kind towards and will have something going. Since you will be making this gesture from your own volition, and not under the pressure of making friends, you will enjoy it, and it will allow you to gain a better perspective of what people want and what they need. Even when your actions do not have the desired effect, you still know that you did your best.

Create Small Talk Around Topics You Enjoy

Small talks are a bore. That much we have established. Often used as a filler for awkward silences, it is often more awkward and bland and often superficial and without direction. For an introvert, who chooses their words carefully, and takes time to think, these kinds of thoughts, of course, makes them want to tear their hair out.

However, while it is indeed true that small talks are mostly terrible, most of it is usually not because of the very concept of small talk, but because very many people out here, both introverts and extroverts, are very terrible communicators. As such, you will find that you are not exactly opposed to small talks as you are to the fact that it will be forced and unnatural.

Therefore, take the time to think of how you would like someone to make small talk with you and where and how. If you are in a position to approach, do it. This approach could be easy to achieve if you attend a function on something you enjoy or consider meaningful.

To do this, take your time. Do not rush into it just because you want to get through it. Give yourself room to grow more comfortable with the idea of going out to strike a conversation.

This point is not to say that you will become someone who will go out and talk to others, but you will know when and how you approach this, thus, still ensuring that you are comfortable with the interaction.

Chapter 9 - Boosting Your Self-Esteem and Shining as an Introvert

Introverts are unique, although there are many people who just don't know what to make of them. You'll usually find them on the perimeter of most parties. People will perceive them as shy, although that's pretty much a mistaken belief. It's just that introverts can only expend so much social energy, and then they need to withdraw and re-energize.

In a world of extroverts, it may be more difficult for introverts to be considered for a promotion, or to make new friends. But it is better that they stay in their introverted lane, because trying to portray themselves as anything else is too hard and would imply not being true to oneself.

Many introverts need to have their self-esteem boosted so that they can shine as exactly who they are. Although this can be a difficult process, it is not impossible.

Being an introvert isn't a character flaw, it's a personality trait, just like being an extrovert. Western society is the more extroverted gung-ho, while Eastern societies have been more accepting of introverts.

Countries such as China, Korea, and Thailand are a haven where introverts are not made to feel inferior; instead, they are perceived as ideal individuals. The inhabitants of such countries believe that being reserved and thoughtful is commendable and indicates good character.

There are Many Ways for Introverts to Shine

Have a positive view of your personality – Don't be ashamed of being an introvert! It's not a flaw, it's a personality trait. Introverts are not alone. Actually, there are more of you than you realize.

Don't be self-critical, and accept the fact that you may find certain things difficult to do. Perhaps talking with strangers is not your strong suit, and speaking in public, in front of an audience, is scarier than the tour of a haunted house. Whatever your weakness is, acknowledge it; don't pile on self-judgement.

Understand your introverted personality – Introverts come in different personality types. The most basic element of introversion is being re-energized by spending time alone or with a close friend who shows you support.

Another fundamental facet is absorbing information before you respond. You want to contemplate what's being told to you. For instance, an extrovert may read an article online and immediately respond and give their opinion about the content. You, on the other hand, want to go away and think about what was in the article before you respond with your opinion. That is, if you decide to give any opinion at all. There's the privacy issue that you enjoy coveting, so sharing what you think may not happen. (Boyes, 2013)

Every introvert is different. You can therefore extract the advice you find helpful and ignore whatever doesn't relate to you.

Don't compare yourself to extroverts – As an introvert, you've probably had a dream and imagined that you're the center of attention, the life of the party. You're the one that everyone listens to as you regale them with your latest adventures about your vacation in Australia, where you went, what you did and who you met.

Even though it seems that being the life of the party wherever you go is great, you should know that being an introvert also has its advantages.

For instance, suppose you published a best-selling novel that turns out to be a hit nationwide, and your publisher informs you that you're going on a book tour. will you enjoy the endless interviews and the spotlight being on you?

If you're an introvert, the previous scenario is not necessarily something you wish to be presented with. If you're really an introvert, you would rather receive the recognition you deserve from a safe distance.

Accept who you are – namely, the person who can read between the lines more carefully than those who get more of the attention. (Hayward, 2018)

The difference between a lack of confidence and being introverted

Confident people have confidence in what they do and how they do it; they also believe that most people will like them. If either of these elements is missing from your confidence bag, it's time to work on it.

Write a blog – Introverts enjoy time alone to ponder their thoughts and jot them down. Today's online blogging world is perfect for introverts to express themselves.

Extroverts are frequently touted for getting out there, but introverts can be impactful through social media, too.

Having a reserved nature can help to build credibility. Our world is where the people shouting the loudest tend to get noticed, while introverts take the time to be observant and make the effort to really listen. Their observations can therefore be translated into pieces of writing that truly touch the audience.

Get creative – Introverts spend quite a bit of time in their own heads, thinking about things they've heard or seen. As previously mentioned, this creativity is great for writing a blog, and it can also unlock other facets of one's personality.

Introverts tend to be more creative. Studies have proved that introverts have the ability to work on their creative projects more thoughtfully than others.

The same studies noted that introverts can work well with others, meaning that you may not necessarily be an artistic spirit, but you'll be able to share good ideas without drowning out the other people involved.

Be a leader and set an example – The notable Forbes magazine points out that some of the best leaders in business, ranging from Bill Gates, the founder of Microsoft, to the super-wealthy investor Warren Buffet, find their time alone to be extremely valuable. The question Forbes addressed is: can the quiet, more reserved businesspeople become illustrious business heads in their own right?

The answer - and the reasons behind it – are as follows: introverted leaders 'think before they speak' and consider what the others are saying. Introverts also react more calmly during a crisis, which can set the example for how the staff will react as well.

A business leader who takes time to re-energize can be more responsive to difficult scenarios and step in rationally rather than reactively.

Avoid the small talk – Introverts are not big talkers when it comes to making new friends or developing romantic interests. This can be misinterpreted as a sign of disinterest. We suppose we have to be friendly and talkative to get the ball rolling with someone new, but you can also get to what you want to talk about without the small talk.

It isn't that you don't have to practice your small talk skills to make communication easier, but you can also get right to the point and talk about what you have on your mind.

There isn't any real need to talk about the headline of the day, or whether it looks like it's going to rain. You can just acknowledge the person by saying "Hi." The conversation will take off from there. No fear, no huge amount of effort to get the conversation going.

Love interests need attention – Introverts have a difficult time when meeting people for the first time. They're quiet and thus project what appears to be disinterest. To counteract this perception, you can let the other person know that you're an introvert from the onset. They might turn out to be an introvert themselves, which could help you feel more relaxed during the date.

Another way to get the date to flow is to ask questions like where they've traveled or what type of books they like to read. Ask the same questions you've been asked by your date as well.

The date is not all about impressing the other party. You're looking to see if you're interested in your date, not if they're interested in you. Remember, the date is a two-way street.

Learn what overstimulates you – Here are a few examples: being asked for an answer and decision while you're focusing on what you want to answer, being interrupted (that's a fan favorite), noisy surroundings, the back and forth of being social, group meetings, and social media – all of it.

Minimize and find ways to work around whatever it is that specifically overstimulates you. Learn physiological self-regulation tactics. (Boyes, 2013)

Physiological Self-Regulation Tactics

These self-regulation tactics can help with stress relief. Their efficiency is confirmed by psychology experts.

You don't have to be exceptional at everything. However, making strides to improve can still be useful. Perfection is not required, and we all know there is no such thing as perfection!

Don't "act extroverted" - Seek ways to team up with others who don't overwhelm and overstimulate you. Understand your tendency to think things through for longer than most other people.

Be conscious of when it's okay to go with your natural propensity versus when you need to supersede it; For instance, try to understand when it's best to make a decision concerning a situation you've been considering for a while. (Boyes, 2013)

Stop the negative self-talk – Don't look at yourself through other people's eyes. Become aware whenever you're comparing yourself with others and stop it.

Develop a positive attitude with positive thinking. Recognize the positive traits you have, develop them further and acquire new ones.

Take note of the negative traits you have (like negative talk about yourself) and eliminate them. That may not be easy at first, so learn to take control of the situation and don't let negative thoughts you back.

Write a list of your positive skills and traits. Remind yourself of these skills by re-reading the list from time to time.

Do positive self-talk once a day, every day. Drown out any negative self-talk you catch yourself doing.

Think about it: Introverts have more opportunities to build healthy self-esteem than extroverts.

Introverts get their mental energy from their inner self – having alone time and contemplating their thoughts and ideas. By contrast, extroverts are driven by outside energy, by connecting with other people.

That being said, extroverts are dependent on other people for their mental energy, while introverts only depend on themselves. The latter also love to delve into self-understanding and self-analysis, thus getting to know themselves better and improving their personality.

Basically, the better you know yourself, the more of an opportunity to improve yourself and gain self-esteem you will have.

There are many extroverts who are good at social networking and use this to their advantage. In today's society, it's important to meet people who study and/or work in your field.

Introverts are extremely self-aware. When they're around people they know well, they're more sociable, thoughtful and gregarious.

Meanwhile, there are some extroverts who waste their time gossiping instead of using the opportunity to build networks as a way to make progress. Extroverts may have social and interpersonal skills, but that doesn't necessarily mean they hold all the cards to be confident.

Self-esteem versus Self-Confidence – Sometimes introverts get confused as to what is self-confidence and what is self-esteem.

Self-confidence refers to the feelings you have about your abilities. These feelings can differ from one situation to the next. For instance, you may have healthy self-esteem and still experience low confidence concerning your math and science skills at school. When you have love for yourself, your self-esteem grows, and that, in turn, makes you more confident.

Someone you know may tell you they don't feel they're good enough and display low self-esteem. They may have been in career positions where they didn't advance or may have been belittled by their supervisor; they may have had toxic personal relationships which ended badly. They're always saying things like "I'm not worth anything."

Acknowledging that this is a negative script is the first step on the path to changing one's attitude.

As for self-confidence, these people may be wonderful, caring friends, who volunteer at animal shelters, adopt pets and ride the neighborhood in search of abandoned and injured animals. They may have submitted their application to study at a top veterinary school, so they can get their degree and work towards opening another animal shelter in order to save and treat more animals. They are confident in their goals and will work hard to achieve them.

As it is, this friend is focusing on the things that they are confident in and working to change their negative self-talk. They are striving to improve both their self-esteem and self-confidence. (Ahmed, 2017)

Adopting a positive attitude and spending time in an environment where you feel positive, with people who are supportive and cheering you on to achieve the goals you've set for yourself will increase your self-esteem and self-confidence.

How to Keep Your Self-Esteem in an Extroverted Society

Introverts do have self-esteem. They are simply less likely to obtain their self-esteem from socializing. They are more apt to get their self-worth from within. This is not true of all introverts, however. (Gaut , 2016)

There are introverts who feel happy knowing that there are no videos of them being drunk and doing stupid things out there; they also take pride in having a small group of trusted friends rather than a big group of acquaintances.

Introverts are usually happy to stay in the background and show little interest in impressing people. However, if they're creative, they are proud to have people notice their creation. That is because their artwork speaks for itself, without requiring any words from the artist.

By comparison, extroverts crave social approval. They want people to like them and some get pretty bothered if someone doesn't like them. Their work is how they display and connect to their personality, and they want their success to be noticed.

Extroverts usually aim at having a large social group, frequently taking pride in being friendly towards wide varieties of people or having the respect of the people within an organization. The persona they display is the foundation of their self-esteem how they are recognized.

Neither personality is right or wrong. Many introverts are proud of the fact they don't need much approval from outside forces, and they have a sense of true self. Extroverts pride themselves in being too self-focused to have rapport with other people and can adapt to the demands of society.

Both personality types have their place, and both need to take care that they don't begin to believe that their side is the only right one. (Gaut, 2016)

Introverts can build their self-esteem and SHINE!

Chapter 10 - The Introvert's Success Plan

It is easier for an introvert to conquer his fears and thrive in the social world if there is a plan that will guide him in his actions. It is also advisable to develop a plan that you can use to start developing your social persona.

Set a goal

Your first task is to set a goal for your social activities. Your goals should be related to the social activities that you have been neglecting in the past. For example, if you have not been on a date for a while, you should make it a goal to go out on dates until you accomplish whatever dating goal you've set for yourself. If you only have a few connections for business, your goal should be to meet someone new related to the industry that you are working for. You should meet someone new every week. The goal that you set depends on the areas of your social life that you have been neglecting in the past.

Embrace your introvert qualities

If you still have negative thoughts about your introversion, you should change them. You should start to enjoy your alone time without guilt. In the social setting, you should be your quiet self and only add to the conversation when you feel comfortable doing so but not going so far as to filter every single thought.

Instead of acting like an extravert all the time, you should limit your use of extravert qualities to important tasks that are important towards your goals.

Chapter 11 - When to Act Like an Extravert?

There are times when you may need to be like an extravert to achieve certain goals. You should do this when doing projects that are important to you or for your loved ones. However, there are certain guidelines that you need to consider, so that you will not be stressed out when you act like an extravert.

Identify the project that you need to work on

First, you need to think about the project that you need to work on. You need to identify the starting and end point of the project. You should also identify the necessary steps that you need to take for the completion of the project.

Learn the required skills

The next thing that you need to do is to identify the extravert skills that you need to use. You may be required to meet new people or to sell something to people. If you are in the business of managing people, you may need to lead them throughout the project.

In some cases, you will be asked to be more outgoing. You will be asked to see more people. There are times when you need to entertain people you barely know. These are not things that introverts usually do but you need to do them for important tasks.

Delegate tasks that you can delegate

If you are in a leadership position, you may want to delegate extravert tasks to true extraverts who are more qualified to do the task based on their personality. You should acknowledge that there are certain tasks that you do not need to do personally.

Do the extravert-tasks yourself if the situation calls for it. There are times when you have no competent extraverts to do the task for you. There may also be times when the tasks are just too important to be delegated.

Keep the experience short

In projects where you need to act like an extravert, you should start early so that you can end the project as quickly as possible. We tire more easily when we are asked to be someone other than our true self. We become conscious of each activity. Sometimes, we may feel awkward. This constant thought on the actions that we take can be taxing to the mind. If you are new into doing an extravert type of task, you may need to finish it as soon as you can to prevent mental fatigue.

Practice the extravert skill that you need to use frequently

There are some extravert-type skills that we need to use regularly for our jobs. For example, if you are into sales, you need to constantly meet new people to gain sales leads. If you are a lawyer, you constantly need to go out to meet clients.

Identify extravert tasks that you need to develop to prosper in your career. You should then put some time into practicing it. Introverts usually take the time to practice their speeches before they actually use them. You may do the same. In sales, for example, companies usually have spiels prepared that their people can recite when selling a product. You do not have to deviate from this spiel when you are just starting out. As you practice the skill, you will become more skilled in the process and your actions will look more natural. Any skill you practice consistently will quickly become second nature.

Find time to unwind after your project

In each project where you need to act like an extravert, you will experience higher stress levels than usual. Because of this, you need to take some time to unwind and to gather yourself in between projects. If you need to do extravert tasks consistently, you may become burned out with the experience because you are not acting like your true self. Getting some alone time in between projects is important to keep your mind healthy.

Chapter 12 - Maximizing Introversion

There are a number of introverts who constantly feel that they are out of place wherever they go, especially at work, public places and sometimes in a group. It is always about who is talking more or who incites the most laugh which is a problem because talking to people and sadly connecting to most of them in a humorous level is not their strongest suit. Often, even before they become a part of a group discussion or work meeting, they have already been typecast as the "loner", quiet, shy and sometimes anti-social person. This social scarlet letter makes it even more difficult for any solitude-seeker to become a well-functioning gear in the group let alone climb the professional ladder. It is becoming clearer to them that success is tailored only to those who can gregariously command attention and forcefully implement at new idea. Brace yourself, though, because things are going to change.

As introverts are becoming more aware of the somewhat favored personalities of the extraverts, they are also realizing that their introversion is not in any way a handicap. It is in fact a very efficient tool and untapped resource that only the taciturns can access—an introverts advantage. The workforce is where every contributing member of the society spends majority of their day. There is no reason why the taciturns cannot make the best of it using their unique innate abilities to maximize its advantage.

Overcome Shyness

The taciturns do not necessarily have a fear of talking to other people outside their circle but it is not rare to find shyness in some. To some you are indeed shy, overcoming it is a task they must face first. Unlike the general public, introverts do not appreciate being thrown into the midst of people and expect for them to learn through survival. They also do not respond well to being "motivated" by force or by threats. To the taciturns, this is a form of attack and another justification why people drain their energy. The best way to tackle shyness is to allow introverts to understand the situation. Questions why and why not should be answered.

Why should you speak? Because you have ideas. In fact, they are better ideas that can help the goals of the company without taking so much risks. You are not aiming to be put on a pedestal for them, you just want to be a contributing part of the workforce and be credited for those contributions accordingly. Have you ever had a situation wherein you refused to convey your ideas and the governing body chose an idea that was so much worse than what you have come up with? Do the words "My idea was better" sound familiar? Not only was this bad idea executed, its loose conception and risk came back to make a terrible impact on everyone else's work—including yours. It is noisy chaos that can be over stimulating for an introvert. If you do not want to speak out for recognition, speak out for the sake of reducing the chaos that disrupts your concentration and solitude.

Speaking to people becomes fearful for some because conversations can lead to casual chat that can jump from one topic to another. Chats are small talks. Small talks change direction also instantaneously to just about anything. Everyone are expected to catch up and to contribute on the different subjects. Introverts are not able to go through this with ease. Not only do they need time to think about what to say, they are also very limited on the "news" or gossips in the office. Nevertheless, communication with people is the desensitizing factor in shyness.

Talk about work. Have a one-on-one conversation with a colleague at the office. The setting is very important because it lets them know that the conversation is about what you are working on and on how he can help. Talking about the job is advantageous for you because as an introvert, you would have already known what the job is all about and any questions pertaining to it you can answer with ease. It also reduces the chances of having small talks. This situation will allow you to control the flow of the conversation unlike when you are in a group meeting where the flow can come from any or every direction thus leaving you overwhelmed. It is this sense of control that you should hold on to.

Now, you may wonder by now, how to handle speaking in front of a crowd. Never fear. You just need to remember the sense of control that you learned in your one-on-one conversation. It may surprise you to know that one-on-one conversations are the hardest for an introvert. Compared to that, speaking in front of a crowd is almost a walk in the park. Why, you ask. It is the control of the flow. When you are speaking, you control the pace of the conversation. You can go slowly and no one would interrupt you or start throwing out small talks at you. As you are speaking about a subject you are an expert on, they can ask questions and you would already have the answers in your head. It is your domain and they are just bystanders. It is an introverts advantage.

Keep Doing What Works

Introverts success is dependent on how the taciturns use their innate abilities to succeed. It is not a secret that introverts learn more through observation, discern without disturbance and productive in solitude. They thrive when they are not surrounded by the constant noise in the office. When other people are satisfied with just looking the superficial aspect of the concept, the taciturns dig further and are relentless in its completion. This is an asset that employers give importance to so maximize it.

Steve Wozniak is probably the biggest supporter of working in solitude and working alone. In his little cubicle in Hewlett Packard, he created the Apple computer which is the pioneer in computer innovation. Until now, he is emphasizing that innovation is rarely achieved in a group. He has a point. Solitude is not just a state for the taciturns. It is a form of protection from the noisy world. It gives them the perfect environment conducive to how their mind works. Without the noise, nothing can disturb their thought process and they become more productive.

Work alone. Keep doing that. As an introvert, there may be countless things in your head that needs to be translated in a way that the people will understand. Disruptions and interruptions does not encourage the thought process to flow and thus must be avoided. Solitude is an enjoyable activity for a taciturn thus in the grand scheme of it all, while you work, you are also enjoying yourself. It is these little life coincidences that can make an introvert successful. This does not mean that teamwork should be abolished. Studies have shown that more influential work have been accomplished compared to what has been done by a group effort. It more of a plea to allow employees to retreat to their private spaces when they need to. Solitude can be a catalyst to excellent performance.

There is no need to advise you to only focus on one work at a time because you had probably already been doing that ever since. Keep doing it. It should not be assumed as being slow but being thorough. You divide the work in manageable sections, tackle and understand each of them and come up with solutions. Determine which of the solutions is best by examining the risks and returns. This is the perfect way to comprehend the work given to you so in any given meeting, you can stand your ground and not be left flabbergasted by questions. Any decent employer will take the quality over the number of their employee's work any day.

Learn as much as you work. This should come easy as one of an introvert's favorite pastime is reading a lot. Keep doing it. Learning constantly will always be a part of the introverts world. Not only is it a source of excitement for many but also a significant tool is success. You will never know what one information can be good for no matter how simple it is. But when the time comes, you know you're ready and fully equipped. The introverts world could possibly be the best place to train and be prepared for anything.

Exude Leadership Material

It is not impossible for an introvert to be an effective leader. In fact, the most influential and successful ones are in some ways introverted. Think Abraham Lincoln and Rosa Parks. But what can you do that can help you become one?

As an employee with seniority, other employees will look up to whether you want it or not. This is an opportunity to show your subtle but effective leadership abilities. Listen to them when they answer questions and avoid interruptions—just like how you would want it if you were talking. Listening is key to good leadership and employees respond well to those who practice it.

Remember your preference for quality conversations instead of quantity. Schedule one-on-one meetings often. These intimate arrangements will allow you to focus on a certain employees and be better acquainted with their capabilities. It is also the best way to promote trust and not make the other introverted employees left out.

Introverts leader supports the proactivity of her employees. By giving them the time to conceptualize new ideas, they function better because they set the pace of the idea themselves. Allow them to run with their ideas and respect their need for solitude when they need it. Unlike introverts, extraverts have the tendency to be threatened by their subordinates' proactivity.

You need to make use of your exceptional writing skills. Make this ability visible on your work perhaps simply through your reports and office memos. For a wider audience, create well-written pieces for the industry publication. You also have the more convenient option of using the social media to get your ideas across. The best part is that you avoid speaking and this the comfort of your home.

Recharge

It speaks for itself. Despite your efforts to be productive and an efficient leader, there will always be a time that you will crave being alone. Do not fight this urge or think of it as a liability or weakness. Solitude is the air that keeps you alive. Without it, there is very little doubt that you will become inefficient in your job. Remember that alone time is also your source of epiphany. So make use of it.

~~~~~

"Did you tire yourself out thinking about it?" It was Bessie.

"Yes."

"Did that make you feel better?"

"A little bit, yes."

"If it bothers you so much, why don't you just apologize?"

"Because I'd have to talk to him again. Isn't that a bit unnecessary unless it's work?"

"Maybe. But you were a bit rude and difficult. People should always be decent enough to apologize."

Difficult. She hates that word. More than she hates the word "shy".

"Fine."

~~~~~

50 How-tos in Becoming a Successful Introvert

Office Pin-Up List

1. Challenge assumptions about you in small ways.

2. Observe and learn the on-goings of the office.

3. Keep yourself up to date with the office news and changes.

4. Make an everyday plan.

5. Be proud of your face. This shows confidence.

6. Always be clean, decent and presentable.

7. Smile.

8. Read. Continuous learning has never been deemed useless.

9. Show up early to meetings to show your commitment.

10. Go to regular meetings. Eventually, they will realize what you can do.

11. Be ready. You never know when you need to step out of your comfort zone.

12. Learn people's names.

13. Do not be afraid to jump back in when you are interrupted.

14. Make your work speak for itself.

15. Excel in tasks especially the one that requires less face time.

16. Show seriousness in your work.

17. Consider having an extrovert to support you.

18. Show your self-esteem by volunteering for jobs that you know you can do.

19. Work alone.

20. Take breaks and recharge when necessary.

21. Do not waste time and energy envying the extroverts.

22. Trust the one-on-one conversation system.

23. Become a sounding board for others.

24. Empathize

25. Extend your helping hand.

26. Fill-in for some small tasks.

27. Keep information so people will not consider you expendable.

28. Think of problems as exciting puzzles on you can solve.

29. Do not be afraid to take credit for your work.

30. Reach out to people in the most comfortable fashion to you.

31. Use technology and social media. It is comfortable interaction.

32. Know your worth.

33. Have something that can absorb your anxiety like a pen you can hold.

34. Breathe. No one will put you in prison for responding in a controlled pace.

35. Don't take it personally. It can be difficult for some extroverts to understand your process.

36. Practice small scale networking.

37. Host an event where you can control the environment.

38. See strangers are friends. Everyone is just as scared as you are.

39. Find a similarity between you and another person.

40. Know and research people you want to meet.

41. Practice the three-second rule. Approach people you think are interesting within three seconds to stop you from overthinking.

42. Practice describing yourself within 30 seconds. Some executives do not have time to listen to long speeches.

43. Create a time limit for conversations. Introverts do not like small talks and extroverts have short attention spans to stay in one.

44. Be mindful of body languages—yours and theirs.

45. Take pictures. It lets you're presence known and a perfect excuse for people to talk to you.

46. Use your own style in speaking.

47. Avoid sounding fake or insincere.

48. Give external hints or body language to let people know how you feel.

49. Celebrate your accomplishments no matter how small they are.

50. Always enjoy your alone time.

~~~~~

Monday.

So I'll tell him I'm sorry and explain why I thought his name was Matthew. Maybe I can add that I was having a bad morning? No, I shouldn't. On my period? That could work. No, no. He might
~~~~~

act weird with the "P" word. Maybe I can ask Bessie to do it for me? No! You're an independent, self-sufficient woman! You can do it. If it ends badly, then you can just pretend he doesn't exist forever or quit. Good plan.

"Coffee?"

"Yes, thank you." She answered almost immediately and took a sip.

"I could have laced that." Marcus said.

Darn. Over thinking makes her less aware of risks.

"But you didn't" She smiled. If I feel the least bit woozy, I'm stabbing you.

"And for that I've decided to forgive you for not knowing my name."

So I don't have to say it? "Thank you."

"How could you not know my name? I'm great!" He said exuberantly.

Ah. Is it getting a little cramped in here? No, it's just your head getting bigger.

"Maybe I should have the name on my door in huge letters?"

Typical extravert. If it makes you feel better about yourself.

"Why not? It will help people like me."

"Maybe later we can go to Henry's Pub for a pint?"

No. I don't think I like you that much.

"What is this 'pub' you speak off?"

"You made a joke... Aw."

This conversation is taking a lot longer than expected. I should have just left the whole thing alone.

"Maybe... but I, uh... sort of promised... my... um..." Now you don't interrupt me?

"Bookshop then?"

Huh. "I'm listening."

"I promise I won't talk to you... I'll just sit on those bean bag things they have in that area of the shop."

"The reading lounge."

"Yes, that one. I'll fend of the creeps lurking around the shop while you browse for hours."

Stay in one place for hours? Wouldn't that kill an extravert? Oh, this could be fun.

"How about you finish those reports and we'll see what happens." I'm sorry but reports need to be finished. I'm just saying.

They both smiled.

You had me at "I won't talk to you."

~~~~~
~~~~~

Chapter 13 Furthering Introvert Creativity

Introverts are naturally creative, and most of you didn't know this. Your ability to assemble and disassemble facts benefits you more than you imagine. Essentially, this is how brilliant ideas are conceptualized and born, making it the greatest edge of introverted people.

Given this fact, it's also important for you to further grow this innate capability because it will benefit you in more than one way. People often think business is about guts and risk-taking, but it also takes a heavy dose imagination to become successful. The same image goes for education. Many believe one should be highly intelligent to progress in this line. What they didn't know is that achievers use their brains to innovate and not merely memorize.

To unleash the greatest potential of your introverted mind, you need to practice habits that can fertilize your creativity. Before you can do so, however, you must recognize obstacles hindering you from achieving this and control them.

Overcoming Creativity Killers

Basically, the primary hindrance to creativity is yourself. You may know the facts of how your mind works, and which areas you progress in, but faith in oneself requires a different approach. This book can repeatedly tell you how brilliant your introverted mind is, but if you don't invest enough trust and faith on yourself, then it will be for naught.

Below are three of the biggest states of mind you should learn to change and tame to unleash your creativity.

1. Thinking you are not creative.

Never think this is limited to those in the artistic line, like painters, sculptors, musicians, and such. Everyone is creative in their own way, and it could be as simple as delivering words. Any novel act you exhibit or thoughts you ponder on requires a certain level of imagination, and you do this everyday -- from the way you converse with others to how you try to predict the outcome of one event.

2. Fear of failure.

You may acknowledge your creativity, and you may come up with many original ideas, but not having enough bravery to act on it will only leave these to waste. Many people didn't push through with materializing their developed concepts because they fear they might fail. It's reasonable to be scared to some level because of its corresponding implications. However, this is also the best thing a person can expect. Failures are not only rich in lessons, but they are also signs of progress. Think of them as a way to see the flaws of your plans or methods. Pin pointing loopholes gives you a chance to further improve them.

3. Being too judgmental.

Excessive critical thinking can kill creativity, because it leads to the belief that ideas will not work even before running them.

Do not mistake this for fear of failure, however. Being too judgmental is almost equivalent to lacking belief in the success of a concept, while the other is lacking belief in the ability of oneself to succeed.

Removing or controlling these barriers is the first move you should make to boost your creativity. The next thing you should know is what practices to adopt.

Cultivating Creativity

Some of the below enumerated are already innate in introverts. However, most of these are practiced unconsciously. Wishing to grow one's creativity requires that these habits to be done knowingly.

1. Continue to seek knowledge.

Information is the primary ingredient of creativity. Coming up with original ideas needs the presence of existing ones, because, as explained earlier, these bits of data are dismantled and reconstructed to gain new perspectives and form innovative concepts.

However, people must also be selective of what knowledge to consume. Take watching television all day, for example. Some may see this as a way to feed themselves with info, and it can, to a certain level. However, looking forward to the events that will unfold to the people of your favorite reality TV show contradicts the purpose.

The best way to learn new things is through active studying, and this does not essentially equate to enrolling in a university. Creativity comes from a combination of a lot of things -- facts, skills, theories, and such. Opting to learn a different language or a musical instrument can be good options.

Remember, however, that the knowledge you gain from this is not limited to the ends itself. Your introverted mind will naturally discern the processes undertaken to reach it, and the data it collects from this is what's necessary. In other words, the means are the ones that hold the ticket to improving your creativity; learning to play a piano, for instance. You don't need to become good at it. What's important is that you understand the mathematical concepts it adapts to produce music. This then is what you can use to combine with other facts to come up with unconventional ideas.

2. Fire up your curiosity.

Never stop in knowing the 'what'. Continue asking and seeking the answers to the 'why', 'where', 'when', 'who', and 'how'. Your brain is like a coin bank. The amount you put in is equivalent to the amount you pull out. In other words, the variety or complexity of your ideas will heavily depend on how much you know.

Following from the example provided in the previous account, aside from examining the means undertaken to learn the piano, there are tons of other information one can opt to gather from this endeavor. Why was the piano invented? How was it conceptualized? Where and when did it originate? Who is the person behind its invention? What material are the strings of the piano made from? How did notes and chords come to life? - And a lot more.

Understand, however, that what separates this from number one is its need for extra effort from you. This will require research. Luckily for you, many of the answers to your possible questions can be found in the internet. The only thing left for you to do is to formulate a question, type it on Google search, and read the entries.

3. There is no such thing as a stupid idea.

Believe it or not, there are successful products out there in the market that were initially considered as dumb. Keep in mind that legends are made when they conquer seemingly crazy endeavors. One good example is the Yellow Smiley Face. This iconic symbol is recognized all over the world, and thanks to this seemingly foolish idea, its creators are now millionaires.

The next time you come up with something, never shut it down because you think it's stupid. Play around with the idea and incubate its potential, because it might just shoot you to success.

4. Read more, listen more, see more, and eat more.

Books, audio, visual works of art, and, yes, food are all products of human imagination. Surrounding yourself with these can induce creativity in you.

5. Don't think of negative reactions from others.

Similar with number three, ideas are commonly dismissed because of the fear of what other people may think. The worst they can give you is their opinion, and these subjective evaluations do not really prove anything except the fact that you can be affected by them.

Furthermore, one can never really predict how others will react. These thoughts, when observed from another perspective, can be considered as mere illusions. To encourage your mind to produce ideas, you need to control and limit these thoughts because they can anchor you to one place.

6. Find similarities between two distinct objects and concepts.

This is a pretty complex mind exercise, but one that guarantees development of a person's creativity. What you do here is select two different objects -- a book and a table for instance. Both are made from wood and they basically hold things (the concept of books is to hold knowledge, while the table, to carry random stuff). Upon realizing these connections, you then explore the possibilities of how tables itself can impart information, and how books can be used to support other objects.

7. Stimulate yourself with the beauty of nature.

Nature can awaken the mind and its senses in ways man-made devices cannot. It can tap in to our deepest being and flood us with inspiration, like how seeing the sunset from the top of the mountain overlooking a peaceful beach can power our spirits. The strength of our minds directly affects our imagination, but emotions can act like fairy dust when applied to it. In other words, your creativity will soar.

8. Logout from time to time.

The revolution of smartphones allowed us to check our email and social media accounts every fifteen minutes. This is not conducive in harnessing your creativity, because it distracts us from contemplation. Rich ideas are incubated in our minds, thus it requires solitude. The interruption and demand for immediate reaction of these platforms takes the mind away from active thinking, and may result in raw and not well-thought-of concepts.

Introverts are creative geniuses by nature, and these tips are merely auxiliary methods should they wish to enhance this trait. It is highly recommended though that you practice these habits should you wish to discover the highest potential of your mind.

Chapter 14 - Introverts and Leadership

Introverts have the capacity to become great leaders as proven by a number of notable and successful figures. Apart from the names enumerated earlier in this book, other known introverted personalities are Abraham Lincoln, Eleanor Roosevelt, Charles Darwin, and Steven Spielberg. The bold and energetic may always take the center-stage, and exhibit confidence when expressing their thoughts, but this does not always translate to effective leadership.

Depending on the structure of the organization, there are companies and nature of businesses where introverts are not well suited. However, the way how most people view extroverts as superior to their more silent counterpart is wrong. The qualities of both personalities are essential in forming a balanced company. Instead of arguing who is a better leader, both parties should make compromises and work together. Nonetheless, the stigma surrounding introverts persists, which makes pointing out their overlapping traits with good leadership necessary.

Without the vocal prowess of extroverts, many believe introverts does not have what it takes to lead, motivate and drive their people. That's actually one good thing about these reserved fellows, they are crafty enough to deviate from the norm and achieve the same, and sometimes even better, results.

Introverted Traits that Makes a Good Leader

1. Good Listeners.

Extroverts follow a single track of thinking, because as explained earlier, they consent to a collectively endorsed predefined set of rules and procedures. Their reactions and decisions are determined by this, making it difficult for them to open up to new ideas most of the time. Introverts, on the other hand, keep their ears open for suggestions, and they think through these ideas.

Nonetheless, compatibility still plays a big role in effectivity and efficiency as a group. According to the study conducted by an associate professor in Harvard School of Business, Francesca Gino, teams with introverted leaders and proactive subordinates can be highly successful. Likewise, bosses who do all the talking are better partnered with passive employees who prefers to be told what to do.

2. Ability to Focus.

Our modern world is full of distractions and concentrating on something can be quite a challenge. With introverts being naturally comfortable with solitude, they aren't afraid to be left with nothing but their minds. Their active thinking sharpens their brain and hones their ability to focus.

In meetings, introverted bosses may sit quietly in the corner, looking indifferent and uninterested, but they are actually processing everything that's being discussed. The amazing thing about them is they not only consume the information being delivered, they theorize, imagine and plan at the same time.

Problems are sometimes debated in the office, and most would often be distracted by the obvious. It's these quiet leaders who often find the solutions because they have the capacity to focus on the issue and look at it from different angles.

3. Humble.

Jane T. Wadell of Regent University conducted a study in 2006 on Servant Leadership. Her research revealed astounding results. She found out that some of the admired traits of Servant Leadership overlap with the inherent traits of introverts, and one of these is humility.

This type of leadership's distinguishing attitude is the way it empowers followers to grow. People bearing these administrative qualities do not fight for the spotlight and aren't driven by egotistic pursuits. They believes that through developing the capabilities of their followers, they achieve the highest potential of their company.

4. Mild Tempered.

As mentioned earlier, extroverts tend to speak as they think. Therefore, whatever they feel at the moment, they will express so. Sometimes, the problem here can be when stress inducing events are encountered, because they can have really bad tempers. This is also because the energy they consume is from their environment. That means if the air is full of heat, they will absorb this and exhibit the same.

Their polar equivalents, on the other hand, are often relaxed and collected. An office in chaos will find order and calm in the presence of an introverted leader, because they feed the atmosphere with their own energy. This quality is overlooked by many and sometimes considered a weakness, but it can be the most powerful asset of an introverted person. You don't easily get carried away by the drama unfolding before you. In fact, you may even have the power to transform these events by exuding the right energy.

5. Creates Meaningful Connections.

In conferences, you will notice who the extroverts are. They are the overly active people who jump from seat to seat talking to different people. Yes, they collect more calling cards than the introverts, but how many of the people they talked to will actually remember they even met? Their counterparts, on the other hand, often limit their interactions to one or two people only, but when they do, they develop a deeper bond.

It is often noted that when someone wants to progress in their career, they need to build their network. Meeting as many relevant people as they can is the initial thought in this endeavor, but what really matters here is the relationship built between the person and their network. You may know Mr. CEO because you chatted with him for five minutes, but this does not mean you are friends already. To categorize this properly, you and Mr. CEO are mere acquaintances. And you don't want to be in the acquaintance-zone because he will barely remember your face, much less your name.

Introverted Traits to Battle to Become a Better Leader

In any given strength is an equivalent weakness. Yes, being an introvert can have its advantages in work and personal life. However, there will always be innate traits bearing the purpose of balancing your seemingly superhero-ish qualities. Most often times, however, these are given more attention by a person, and they tend to mingle too much on these that it overshadows the positive ones.

Reminding you what they are can help you tame them, and let your introverted superpowers shine.

1. Leave your comfort zone.

Introverts prefer working alone because this is how they function best. Their thinking is maximized, and their creativity is heightened, thus solitude gives them comfort. However, leadership requires constant interaction with subordinates. Putting themselves out there can be a bit difficult and awkward, but it is necessary to become a better leader. One cannot solely rely on their brain power. Success also takes teamwork.

2. Speak your thoughts.

There are times when introverts get too deep in thought they forget to speak. Your ideas may be difficult to explain because it can get too complex for other people to understand, but still, these needs to be expressed. In a workplace under chaos, these might just be the solution the management needed. Besides, when everyone else is panicking, you might be the only one who is calm enough to concentrate on the situation and speak with sense.

Chapter 15 - Getting Ahead in Business

There are institutions that heavily require the vocal and outgoing traits of extroverts, such as networking companies and brokerage firms. However, with the rise of the digital age, the qualities of introverts are beginning to play a more significant role in the market.

Unlike before when communication is done one-way and encourages little to no interaction, the digital platform enables people to engage by sharing content. This requires thoughtfulness, and an approach that invites people to participate. With the given qualities of introverts, they are destined to succeed as marketers of the future.

1. Meaningful Content.

Many businesses are shifting from traditional face-to-face selling to online marketing. Not only do they save a hefty amount of cash, they reach a wider audience. This, however, causes congestion on the internet.

Hundreds to thousands of advertisements flash, pop, glitter, and do different kinds of exhibition to get your attention. These gather the attention of anyone much like how an extrovert does, but these can be easily ignored, especially from behind the computer because people can opt to be indifferent and judgmental. What makes an effective marketing campaign in the digital platform is content.

Introverts happen to have an edge in this area. They listen, observe, and process information that enables them to produce highly insightful and thoughtful content that can hold anyone's attention. People are then encouraged to engage in the campaign by sharing, liking, retweeting, and such.

2. Straight to the Point Messages.

Businesses are about sending messages. This is always the first step to induce curiosity among potential clients. However, with the internet getting intensely cluttered, the attention of audiences has evolved to be limited to micro-seconds. Extroverts would often initiate communication via small talks, and apply the same strategy in online marketing. However, most people avoid these if they can, and again, from their comfortable seats at home, they can. Introverts can heavily relate to this. They dislike small talks; that's why they get straight to the point. Messages that immediately speak out what they want people to know often get more quality attention.

3. Stronger Relationships.

If extroverts are focused on getting "dates", their polar equivalents are poised to build "marriages" in the digital platform. This means they are more willing to engage and respond to whatever point of view presented by readers after sharing a content, whereas their counterparts are commonly satisfied with getting mere likes. In our modern world, connection plays a more significant role than reach, and introverts are the point persons when aiming to build this both in real life and online.

4. Initiates and Values Collaboration.

It's common to encounter in the internet contents that exude individualistic messages. There are some marketing campaigns out there that focus so much light on themselves, not knowing they turn off most people than stimulate them. Introverts, on the other hand, believe in the power of collaborative work. They recognize that combined efforts of thinkers and multiple players can produce moving messages and grander results.

5. Willingness to Share Content of Others.

A healthy online ecosystem revolves around giving and taking. Marketers can gain wider audiences and deeper credibility by sharing meaningful contents posted by others -- of course, containing full details of where it came from and who owns the copyright. Between the two personality types, introverts are more open to this idea, and they may even initiate the act.

6. Authenticity and Transparency.

It's easy to spot lies online and this is the secret ingredient in inducing doubt among internet users. Introverts, on the other hand, are very transparent in their messages and they never glitter their words. In simpler terms, what you see is what you get. They don't hide anything under the rock, and they don't have any reason to.

Business isn't always done face-to-face. With the advent of technology, introverts can opt to stay within the comforts of their homes and still perform as effectively as their extroverted counterparts in business. As often taught by many successful people, take advantage of the things you are good at, and utilize them well to meet your objectives. You don't always have to follow what everyone is doing. Introverts are crafty enough to deviate from the norm and pave their own ways through unconventional methods. The only thing you need is to properly equip yourself with knowledge, and by reading this book, you already have.

There is no special ingredient to gain power, because it's already inherent in you. Your powerful introverted mind only needs to realize its capabilities and, of course, belief in oneself to unleash its highest potential.

Chapter 16 - Benefit from Your Relationships

According to the longest study on happiness - a 75-year old study on adult life -the key to a happier and healthier life is having good relationships. This may seem bad news for an introvert who barely keeps in touch with one or two of his friends. Fortunately, it is not about the number of our friends we have, but about the quality of our relationships. With this, we are actually at an advantage. Introverts are experts in cultivating deep and lasting relationships.

However, though we possess traits advantageous to a good relationship, we also have those that harm it. We have to discern whether we are strengthening our relationships or destroying them.

Which traits benefit your relationships?

Being a good listener—People normally want to talk about themselves, even introverts, but rarely find someone who really listens. That is why good listeners are valued friends, especially for an introvert who always does the listening.

Youraptitude for deep conversations—Deeper conversations leads to deeper connections. Even an extrovert appreciates a meaningful conversation. They can open up about serious topics because they know they will be taken seriously. Researchers also found that the happiest people are those who have more meaningful conversations over small talk.

Your contemplative nature– Because you think before you speak, you rarely regret what you say. Continue to be cautious of your words because careless words can heavily damage even the closest relationships.

Your preference for a smaller group of friends –Fewer friends guarantees intimacy and loyalty. Besides, humans are only capable of maintaining a few intimate relationships. That is why some friendships end when new ones begin. The fewer you friends you have, the longer you keep them and the more valuable they become. Introverts are also naturally loyal to the few friends they have.

Which traits harm your relationships?

Passive listening–Sometimes, when we get so wrapped up in listening or contemplation, we forget to respond to the person talking. Add some interjections to show that you are listening.

Reticent nature–Being reserved is not a bad thing, but sometimes, we leave too many things unsaid, even words that show our affection. Get out of your comfort zone. There are times when you should compromise for the sake of the people important to you.

Avoiding confrontations–This may keep the peace for a while, but it is silently corroding your relationship. This is another occasion where you have to step out of your comfort zone. Confrontations can always be done calmly and rationally.

Tendency to be too critical and judgmental–Our judgmental tendencies and reluctance to open up hinder us from making new friends. Remember that not all our judgements are accurate. Give people the benefit of the doubt. Most of the time, we end up befriending the least person we expect.

Being suddenly out of reach–Give your friends a heads-up whenever you plan on recharging your batteries. Your extroverted friends may not understand if you don't explain the need for it because for extroverts, being alone give the opposite effects.

Enjoy casual socializing

It is true that introverts are drained by socializing, but it is also true that we enjoy the time spent with others. A conversation with a nice stranger or a cheerful cashier can liven up our mood. Researchers found that acting assertive or being more talkative can result to positive emotions, even for an introvert.

Just like everyone else, we become happier when we socialize. The only difference is we are drained of energy whereas extroverts are recharged. So how can we benefit from socializing? Do we have to be drained every time we want to feel happy?

Here are some ways you can be socially connected without the compromise:

Find like-minded individuals - Spending time with another introvert is less taxing because you understand each other's limitations and sensitivities.

Strike-up short but meaningful conversations - Walk up to the store clerk and ask about her day. Initiating the conversation is being assertive.

Make time and effort for the people closest to you - Their presence can make you comfortable and confident of who you are. Since they have accepted the way you naturally are, so should you.

Read a blog or a book - Though this is a solitary activity, you get the social connection you need. It can even be more intimate than a short conversation. Through reading, you get to see a person's inner thoughts and feelings.

Application:

Go out this weekend and spend some time with that friend whom you haven't seen for some time.

Strike up a conversation with someone you don't know. He can be the cab driver or your favorite barista. Practice having short but meaningful conversations.

Conclusion

Remember that your introversion is normal. It is not a disorder that needs immediate treatment. It is a part of our genetics. Hence, even if we develop extroverted behaviors, we will always be introverted deep inside.

Identifying your limitations is essential in overcoming them. Sometimes, you can use even those traits that have set your limits to your advantage.

Keep in mind that shyness and introversion are different things. Introversion is something we have to embrace to accept who we are. On the contrary, extreme shyness is something we have to overcome. To overcome it, you must uproot it from your core.

After identifying your strengths and limitations, use them to your advantage. Focus on your traits that will help you excel in work and those that strengthen your relationship. Excelling in your work and having good relationships are keys to a more fulfilling life.

I hope this book was able to help you to overcome the limitations that have been prohibiting you from reaching the success and happiness you want and deserve!

The next step is to take action! Every day, you should be applying what you've learned here.